Twayne's United States Authors Series

Sylvia E. Bowman, *Editor*

INDIANA UNIVERSITY

Benjamin Penhallow Shillaber

Benjamin Penhallow Shillaber

by JOHN Q. REED

Kansas State College of Pittsburg, Kansas

 **209**

Twayne Publishers, Inc.   : :   New York

For
Mary, Barbara, and Jack

PREFACE

BENJAMIN P. Shillaber is not a major American author, but he does deserve more consideration than he has thus far received from scholars and critics. As journalist, editor, humorist, and lecturer, he left his mark upon the times in which he lived, and he merits at least a place in the ranks of minor American writers. It is my hope that this book will arouse some interest in the man and his work and serve as a basis for future research and criticism. Since this study is the first extended one of Shillaber and his writing, I have probably made some errors in fact and judgment; but I sincerely hope that these are minimal.

My own interest in Shillaber stems from extensive research which I did some years ago on Charles Farrar Browne, better known as Artemus Ward. The fact that Browne's first known humor was published in the *Carpet Bag* led to an interest in the magazine and that, in turn, to my interest in Shillaber, its editor. Finding that Shillaber's life and work had received little scholarly or critical attention, I resolved to do some pioneering work on him; and this book is the result of my investigation.

My basic purpose in the book is critical rather than biographical; but, since the facts of Shillaber's life are not well known, I have summarized the scanty biographical information available. Although I have analyzed his lectures, his books for boys, and his popular verse and fiction, I have placed my emphasis upon his humor because his literary reputation must ultimately rest upon his humorous writing. I have attempted to analyze the techniques and values of his humor, to relate it to the native comic tradition, and to show that he possessed more versatility as a humorist than has generally been assumed.

Since Shillaber's work is out of print and since few readers have much acquaintance with it, I have quoted extensively both from his own collections of his writings and from those buried in the files of newspapers and magazines. I have selected pieces which are both representative and of high quality. And, in this regard, I wish to thank the librarians in Porter Library and the many librarians over the country who helped me secure copies of Shillaber's letters and his uncollected writings. I am particularly indebted to Philip J. McNiff of the Boston Public Library for making available microfilm copies of the Boston *Post* and to Biagino M. Marone of the Wisconsin State Historical

Society for arranging to have the Boston *Saturday Evening Gazette* put on microfilm for me. I would also be ungrateful not to mention my debt to my colleagues, Dudley T. Cornish, Gene DeGruson, Tom Hemmens, and Rebecca Patterson for reading and criticizing my manuscript and for rendering other valuable assistance. Finally, I am grateful to Sylvia E. Bowman for encouraging me to undertake this study and for her editorial help in completing it.

Pittsburg, Kansas

JOHN Q. REED

CONTENTS

CHRONOLOGY

1814   Benjamin Penhallow Shillaber born, Portsmouth, New Hampshire, July 12.

1830   Began his apprenticeship as a printer on the New Hampshire *Palladium* in Dover.

1833   Went to Boston where he worked as a printer for Tuttle and Weeks.

1836   Sailed in October to Demerara, British Guiana, where he worked as a printer on the *Royal Gazette*.

1838   Returned to Boston where he again worked for Tuttle and Weeks. Married Ann Tappan de Rochemont on April 15.

1840   Went to work as a printer on the Boston *Post*.

1847   Published first Mrs. Partington squib in the *Post* on February 26 and became a member of the reportorial staff of the *Post*.

1850   Joined the staff in Boston of the *Pathfinder and Railway Guide*.

1851   Became part owner and coeditor of the *Carpet Bag;* first issue of the magazine appeared March 29.

1853   Returned to the Boston *Post* as local reporter; published *Rhymes With Reason and Without*.

1854   *Life and Sayings of Mrs. Partington*.

1855   Moved to Chelsea; made his debut as a public lecturer on December 13.

1856   Became associate editor of the Boston *Saturday Evening Gazette*.

1857   Lecture tour through the South and Middle West.

1859   *Knitting Work: A Web of Many Textures, Wrought by Ruth Partington*.

1863   *Mrs. Partington's Ridicule*.

1867   Left the *Saturday Evening Gazette*.

1873   *Partingtonian Patchwork*.

1874   *Lines in Pleasant Places*.

1879   *Ike Partington; or, The Adventures of a Human Boy and His Friends*.

1880   *Cruises With Captain Bob on Sea and Land*.

1882   *The Double-Runner Club; or, The Lively Boys of Riverton,* and *Wide-Swath.*
1883   Wife died.
1888   *A Midnight Race.*
1890   Mrs. *Partington's New Grip-Sack, Filled With Fresh Things.*
1892   Died on November 25.
1893— Mrs. *Partington's Grab Bag* published.
1894   "Experiences During Many Years" published serially in *New England Magazine.*

Benjamin Penhallow Shillaber

CHAPTER 1

A Provincial Among the Brahmins

WHEN Seba Smith introduced Major Jack Downing to American readers in the pages of the Portland (Maine) *Daily Courier* in January, 1830, he inaugurated a productive native literary movement which was to retain its vigor throughout the remainder of the century.[1] Although Seba Smith's hero had a number of literary ancestors, including Benjamin Franklin's "Poor Richard," Jack Downing was the first fully drawn common-sense philosopher in American humor. Partly, at least, because of the emphasis placed on the sagacity of the common man during the age of President Andrew Jackson, Jack Downing was immensely popular, and his success encouraged a number of other newspaper humorists to create similar comic characters. One of the most important humorists to follow the lead of Seba Smith was Benjamin Penhallow Shillaber, who created in Mrs. Partington not only a very popular and firmly conceived female counterpart to Jack Downing but also a significant and enduring figure in American humor.

I *Birth and Boyhood in New Hampshire*

Of the early life of Benjamin P. Shillaber, we know very little.[2] Born in Portsmouth, New Hampshire, on July 12, 1814, he was one of six children born to William Shillaber and his second wife Sarah. He was descended from John Shillaber, who had emigrated from England in 1688 after being involved in the Monmouth Rebellion. Both of Benjamin's grandfathers had served in the American Revolution: Joseph Shillaber, his paternal grandfather, was an armorer under John Paul Jones on the *Bonhomme Richard;* and Joseph Sawyer, his maternal grandfather, had been wounded in the war. Benjamin may have inherited his Yankee wit from Eunice Cutts Sawyer, his maternal grandmother; for he remembered that, after her husband had died and she had left her old home at Spruce Creek, when it was reported to her that her house must be haunted because bright lights were often seen in it, she replied, "It cannot be haunted by my husband because he was always too saving of lights to indulge in such extravagances." [3]

Portsmouth, Shillaber's birthplace and the city in which he spent his youth, had a long history, having been founded in 1623 and incorporated as a town in 1653. A pleasant city located on the Piscataqua River, it contained a number of handsome colonial houses which gave it a distinctive air of antiquity. It had been a prosperous city, but by the time of Shillaber's birth it was losing ground, in part at least, because of the removal of the state capital to Concord in 1808. Although Shillaber spent most of his life in Boston, he never lost his affection for Portsmouth, and he incorporated many of his happiest boyhood memories of his native city into his verse and his books for boys. In verses composed to be read at a Fourth of July celebration in Portsmouth in 1853 he wrote:

> And memories, like railway trains
> Come freighted, full, of Portsmouth Plains—
> That greater field, in Boyhood's view,
> Than New Orleans or Waterloo!
> With mighty deeds of arms 'tis rife,
> And rattling drum and squeaking fife,
> And Berri's bunns, and weary legs,
> And apple juice, and hard-boiled eggs! [4]

Shillaber attended the West School in Portsmouth until 1830 when he was sixteen; then, like many other American humorists and writers, he continued his education as an apprentice in a newspaper office. He served more than two and one-half years of his apprenticeship on the New Hampshire *Palladium* in Dover; and, when this paper failed, he went to Boston in 1833 at the age of eighteen. Except for two years in South America, he lived and worked in Boston for the rest of his life.

II *Printer in Boston and British Guiana*

On a chilly spring morning in May, Shillaber took the stagecoach from Portsmouth to Boston. After arriving toward evening at the Eastern Stage House, he found lodging in a boardinghouse on Union Street, where he remained for several months before moving to another one. No doubt his experience of living in a succession of Boston boardinghouses prompted him later to use a boardinghouse table as the setting for a number of his humorous anecdotes.

Within a short time after arriving in Boston, Shillaber went to work for Tuttle and Weeks, a book-printing firm on School Street, where he completed his apprenticeship as a printer. Tuttle and Weeks, one of the larger and more important printing establishments in Boston, printed, among other things, Thomas G. Fessenden's *The New England Farmer,* Lydia Maria Child's *Anti-Slavery Annual,* and Samuel G. Goodrich's very popular "Peter Parley" books for children. Always a gregarious man, Shillaber soon made the acquaintance of a number of the lesser literary figures of Boston. The Old Corner Bookstore on Washington Street, then operated by John Allen and William D. Ticknor, provided a considerable amount of printing for Tuttle and Weeks, and Shillaber soon became acquainted with several of the editors and writers connected with the publications of this firm. The most enduring friendship which he made at this time was with James T. Fields, also a native of Portsmouth who was then employed by the firm of Allen and Ticknor. Fields, who later became a partner with William D. Ticknor in the illustrious publishing house of Ticknor and Fields, encouraged Shillaber for many years in his literary endeavors; but for some reason his firm was never to put its imprint on one of Shillaber's books. The fact that the publishers of Henry Wadsworth Longfellow, James Russell Lowell, Oliver Wendell Holmes, Ralph Waldo Emerson, Henry David Thoreau, and Nathaniel Hawthorne refused to publish his work was a lifelong disappointment to Shillaber.

Shillaber attended lectures, visited all of the patriotic shrines in the vicinity of Boston, became a devotee of the theater, and developed an avid interest in the history of Boston. He also took the keenest interest in American politics, the course of which was to be dominated for more than a generation by the issue of slavery. One memorable event which occurred during his early years in Boston was the visit which President Jackson and his entire cabinet made to the city on June 30, 1833. An ardent admirer of Jackson, Shillaber remained loyal to the concepts and principles of Jacksonian democracy for the remainder of his life. In 1836, when he was old enough to vote for the first time in a presidential election, he cast his vote for Martin Van Buren, the Democratic candidate; and, until his death, Shillaber remained a strong, even militant, supporter of the Democratic party.

Shillaber was always to remember, too, the mobbing in Boston in 1835 of William Lloyd Garrison, publisher of the *Liberator,* the nation's most influential Abolitionist newspaper. He was also deeply impressed by the excitement and bitterness which accompanied the presidential campaign of 1840, the campaign in which the victor, William Henry Harrison, ran as the "log-cabin, hard-cider candidate." Shillaber was to recall vividly, too, the mile-long Whig procession up Bunker Hill in 1840 to dedicate the monument to the famous battle fought there in 1775 and the amusement of Boston Democrats when the parade was suddenly terminated by a heavy rainstorm which forced Daniel Webster, Edward Everett, Rufus Choate, and the other distinguished party leaders to scurry for cover in a most undignified manner. Although Shillaber never became an active politician himself, his ardent interest in politics and politicians continued throughout his long life.

During his early years in Boston, Shillaber began to attend the Reverend Hosea Ballou's Universalist church, which was located near the printing establishment of Tuttle and Weeks. Ballou was then the foremost leader of the denomination, the distinctive belief of which was that all men would finally be saved. Although there is no conclusive proof that Shillaber was actually a member of the Universalist denomination, he certainly shared the optimistic view of life and death espoused by the Universalists, and he apparently maintained some connection with the church for the remainder of his life. On June 28, 1872, nearly forty years after he first arrived in Boston, he read original verses at a Universalist meeting in Faneuil Hall in which he rejected the pessimistic tenets of Calvinism and endorsed the optimism of Universalist beliefs:

> We have deep sympathy for such as cling to dogmas
>   dismal,
> Who smell, in all life's pleasant things, an
>   atmosphere abysmal,
> Who, with unhealthy fancies fraught, sigh o'er their
>   neighbor's errors,
> And see in all God's attributes no features but his
>   terrors,—
> Consigning those not of their fold to Satan's dark
>   dominion,
> While theirs shall pass the ordeal, and never scorch
>   a pinion:
> With tastes all warped to match their souls, by
>   bigotry incrusted.
> Well was it that to any such the earth was not
>   intrusted—
> To mould it and to decorate—there'd be no cheerful
>   feature,
> And mirth would be a tabooed thing in every living
>   creature.[5]

These lines express the cheerfulness and optimism which dominated Shillaber's life and which are constant throughout his writing. This optimism, although it may often seem superficial and excessive to the modern reader, nevertheless sprang from deep convictions which Shillaber held concerning the nature of man and the universe; but such an optimistic attitude was also characteristic of the age in which he lived.

In the winter of 1835 Shillaber gave up boardinghouse life and moved to the south end of the city to live with the Tappan de Rochemont family; he became acquainted with Ann Tappan de Rochemont, who later was to be his wife. In October, 1836, while living in the Tappan de Rochemont home and pursuing his work as a printer, he suffered a severe nasal hemorrhage, and his physician advised him that he must live in a warmer climate if he expected to recover. Fortunately, Tappan de Rochemont, his future brother-in-law, was then visiting his family, and he suggested that Shillaber accompany him to British Guiana where he had been living for several years. Within a short time the two men sailed for Georgetown, the capital of British Guiana, where Shillaber met John Baum, one of the publishers of the *Royal Gazette,* who offered him a job as a printer for the newspaper which was published in Demerara and which was the official organ of the British government in the colony. Shillaber accepted the position at once, and for twenty months he served as a compositor on the *Gazette.* The *Gazette,* which was issued triweekly, carried little news of consequence, most of its space being devoted to verbatim reports of the proceedings of the legislature.

Although Shillaber enjoyed his work on the newspaper, he found life in Demerara generally dull and uneventful. The only excitement which he recalled years later was that which followed the death of William IV in 1837 and the succession of Victoria to the British throne. Since his health was restored and since he was also quite homesick, he gladly returned to Boston in July, 1837, where he again worked as a printer for Tuttle and Weeks. On August 15, 1838, after a short courtship, he married Ann Tappan de Rochemont, the daughter of the family with which he had lived prior to his stay in British Guiana. Benjamin and Ann Shillaber were to be the parents of eight children of which only four, one boy and three girls, grew to adulthood. The couple lived very happily together until Ann's death forty-five years later.

III *The Boston* Post

Since his marriage had increased his need for money and since Tuttle and Weeks paid him very modest wages, Shillaber searched for a more lucrative situation. In 1840, through the help of George F. Emery, an old friend from Portsmouth, Shillaber secured a position on the Boston *Post,* one of the country's leading newspapers. Edited by Charles Gordon Greene, the *Post* had been founded in 1831 as an organ of a radical faction of the Democratic party in Massachusetts led by David Henshaw.[6] From the beginning, the newspaper had supported the cause of the workingman against the menace of the new industrialism in New England. Greene himself was a personable and capable man and an influential leader in the Democratic party whose allegiance to the party was proudly proclaimed by a bust of Andrew Jackson over the door of his office and by a slogan under the masthead of the paper which carried Jackson's famous words, "The Union—It Must Be Preserved."

But the *Post* was much more than an organ of the Democratic party; it was also an excellent newspaper, attractive and well edited. In addition to news and intelligent, though strongly partisan, editorials, the *Post* encouraged the cultural life of Boston. Reviews of current theatrical productions, lectures, concerts, and operas were regular features of the newspaper. Book reviews, too, had a prominent place in the pages of the *Post,* and these were generally of high quality. In addition, the newspaper, which had a strong literary bent, regularly carried verse by popular writers such as John G. Saxe and Lydia H. Sigourney; and, after Shillaber became a member of its writing staff, it printed generous amounts of his poetry.

Since Greene was an influential man, numerous people of importance came to confer with him in his small, crowded office. George Bancroft, the historian, often dropped in to compliment him on an editorial. Caleb Cushing, then congressman from Massachusetts and later attorney general of the United States, also visited frequently, as did Horace Greeley, Franklin Pierce, and Nathaniel Parker Willis. Although Shillaber did not meet all of Greene's distinguished visitors, he received considerable satisfaction from seeing them come and go.

It is difficult to determine exactly what Shillaber's duties on the *Post* encompassed before 1847 when he created Mrs. Partington and became a journalist as well as a printer. Except for a few contributions to "All Sorts of Paragraphs," a personal column, he apparently did little writing, but after 1847, this column seems to have become one of his chief responsibilities, and he made it one of the most popular features of the *Post.* In addition to the Mrs. Partington sketches, the column included anecdotes, aphorisms, light verse, notes on lectures and concerts, comments on politics, and national news items. Altogether it was lively, entertaining, and informative.

Without doubt Shillaber's chief interest in his column was in reporting and commenting on national, state, and local politics. As evidenced by his comments in "All Sorts of Paragraphs," his political principles were clearly and consistently those of the Democratic party. He read the exchanges and reported in great detail on Democratic victories in state and local elections all over the United States, and he carried on a running feud with the *Whig* and the *Atlas,* the two leading Whig newspapers of Boston. It is true that, since the *Post* was a Democratic newspaper, Shillaber had no choice except to support the party; but we are firmly convinced as we read his columns that his enthusiasm for the party was sincere and that he believed whole-heartedly in the political principles of Jefferson and Jackson. To Shillaber, democracy and the Democratic party were synonymous. Fervently egalitarian, he expressed repeatedly his belief in the importance of the common man and in the absurdity of an aristocracy of rank and privilege in a democratic nation. "To have had eminent ancestors," he wrote in the *Post,* "is not half so great a blessing as to have had *honest* ones; for moral qualities are transmissible in the blood, which titles and station are not." [7] He opposed the Whig party because, in his opinion, it represented the selfish interests of the wealthy and powerful and had, therefore, no concern for the welfare of the lower economic classes. Commenting on a Whig rally which was held in Boston for Gen. Zachary Taylor, Whig candidate for the presidency in 1848, Shillaber wrote:

It was a sorry sight to see many well looking working men from out of town adding their strength to the grand humbug and claptrap the other evening of the Boston aristocracy. If they knew the estimation in which they were held by the wire pullers of the movement they would have staid at home, and not made themselves the tools of a party as dead to any feeling of sympathy for them as they are dead to anything like self-respect. It is no place for a working man in such a mess, and to find them there shows either a want of understanding on their part, or a reckless indifference for their country's weal; either way arguing ill for themselves. [8]

In a city noted for its conservatism, its Brahmin caste, and its genteel culture, Shillaber championed the cause of the laboring classes against the privileged orders. Like many other contemporary Democrats, he displayed openly and proudly his sympathy for the common man and his distaste for the aristocratic and genteel by affecting a very careless manner of dress. One of his contemporaries commented on his appearance at this time: "Should the reader meet him in the street, he would take him for an unsophisticated back-woodsman, and not for one of the editors of one of the most influential journals in the United States." [9]

In the light of Shillaber's strong Democratic leanings and his sympathy for the common man, we can see clearly that his creation of Mrs. Partington was not an accident. A representative of the common people, she is unlettered, provincial, and ignorant of the conventions of genteel society; but she is nevertheless good and kind and possessed of a large fund of natural or folk wisdom which makes her the equal if not, indeed, the superior of the Boston aristocracy.

In 1847, when Shillaber began to write for the *Post,* the dominant political issue was the Mexican War, which had begun in May, 1846. Shillaber, as we might expect, saw the conflict as a just one; and he vigorously defended President Polk's prosecution of the war. Again and again in his column he attacked the Whigs because of their opposition to the war. When James Russell Lowell's *The Biglow Papers* appeared, Shillaber disagreed strongly with the antiwar sentiments expressed in them and dubbed Lowell a spokesman for the Whigs.[10] In the 1848 presidential campaign, Shillaber championed Lewis Cass, the Democratic candidate; and, after Cass was defeated, he repeatedly criticized the spoils system of the new administration. He was particularly incensed when Nathaniel Hawthorne was removed by the Whigs from the office of Surveyor of Salem. Of Hawthorne's removal he wrote, "The 'essential prerequisites' of 'honest capacity and fidelity' were undeniably possessed by him; had they been possessed in an equal degree by the present administration, Mr. H. would not have been proscribed." [11]

On the overwhelming issue of slavery Shillaber and the *Post* took the general position assumed by most Northern Democrats. Although he had no enthusiasm for slavery, he opposed the Abolitionists. Like many other Democrats, he took this position because of his Jeffersonian fear that the issue of slavery would lead to a division of the Union. The fanaticism of the leaders of the Abolitionist movement disturbed him greatly and led him to attack them again and again. "The Abolition Leaders," he wrote in the *Post* in 1847, "it will be seen by the report of the proceedings of the anti-slavery convention have lost none of their powers of unsparing abuse of all who do not run on all fours with them, or of applying scurrilous epithets to those who are known to be opposed to their treasonable projects." [12] Like most Northern Democrats, he was opposed to the extension of slavery into new territory, but he favored a policy of popular sovereignty rather than the Wilmot Proviso because he believed that it was unconstitutional for the federal government to prohibit slavery.[13]

It was Mrs. Partington, however, rather than his political views which made Shillaber one of the best-known newspapermen of his day. Mrs. Partington first appeared in the column "All Sorts of Paragraphs" on February 26, 1847, in a quip in which Shillaber complained about the taste of the city water. In a postscript to the squib he wrote, "Mrs. Partington insists that she will have to put *alkali* into her tea to destroy the taste of the *ile*." Her name, he said, he borrowed from Sydney Smith, the English clergyman and essayist, who had used it in a famous speech delivered in 1831 at Taunton, England, in which he had castigated the privileged classes for their opposition to progress. To underscore the futility of the opposition of the aristocracy to the great reform movement which was under way at that time, Smith had included in his speech an anecdote about a Mrs. Partington of Sidmouth who, during a great storm, attempted to sweep back the Atlantic Ocean with her broom.[14]

It was not until June 5, 1847, that the second Mrs. Partington piece appeared in the column. The short anecdote was inspired, Shillaber said, by a nonsensical remark made by a man one night when the news came from England that the price of flour had increased. The man remarked that the higher price did not matter to him since he bought his flour by the pound. Shillaber's squib was as follows: "Mrs. Partington says that she has always noticed that, whether flour was dear or cheap, she invariably had to pay the same money for a half dollar's worth."

This bit of humor was widely copied the following morning by other newspapers, and the long career of Mrs. Partington was under way. Colonel Greene promoted Shillaber, and he wrote a series of anecdotes concerning Mrs. Partington. These were reprinted by newspapers all over the country, and Shillaber achieved national popularity as a humorist. He later added Mrs. Partington's nephew Ike to the Partington sketches, and he too made a hit with the public. Old Roger, Wideswarth, and Digby, three other humorous characters with which he experimented, were substantial literary creations, but they were not nearly so popular with readers as Mrs. Partington and Ike.

Shillaber continued to work on the *Post* until 1850, when he left to join the staff of the *Pathfinder and Railway Guide*. This publication, which was published by Wilder, Pickard, and Company, carried—in addition to railway schedules—news and short humorous sketches which were intended to amuse its readers. Since it was financed by advertisers and distributed gratuitously to railway passengers, the little sheet had a wide circulation and reached many readers. His tenure on the *Pathfinder* was short because early in 1851 he left to become a part owner and coeditor of the *Carpet Bag,* a new magazine which was to be devoted to publishing humorous writing.

IV   *The* Carpet Bag

Although the publication of an exclusively comic magazine had never been attempted in the United States, Shillaber and his partners, Silas W. Wilder, Charles G. Halpine, and John T. Trowbridge, felt confident that such a publication could succeed. Pooling their talent and resources, the four men determined to launch a magazine devoted entirely to humor; and on March 29, 1851, the first issue of the *Carpet Bag* appeared.[15] Published weekly, the magazine was an eight-page folio with an appealing format. The purpose, according to a statement made by its editors in the first issue, was "to make it an agreeable fireside and wayside companion, affording both amusement and instruction. . . . The name *Carpet Bag* we have adopted as expressing the miscellaneous character of a good paper, into which are crowded a variety of things necessary for the comfort and happiness of the highways of life. . . . One of the prominent features of the *Carpet Bag* will be to promote cheerfulness. Not that we shall try to be exclusively funny, ever toiling to pick up something that shall make the vulgar laugh; but a good joke or a pleasant satire or a harmless witticism we shall welcome to our columns." [16]

Politically the magazine was nonpartisan, and what little satire it contained was generally genial and inoffensive. Although its writers poked fun at contemporary fads like spirit rapping and bloomers for women, they carefully avoided the more serious and controversial issues of the day. The one time that the magazine did become involved in a serious controversy was during the Scott-Pierce presidential contest in 1852, but involvement in the incident backfired and damaged the circulation of the magazine. As a means of satirizing the contest, the staff of the magazine had entered an imaginary, nonpartisan candidate named "Ensign Jehiel Stebbings" into the campaign. Ensign Stebbings, who was conceived by Benjamin Drew, was ostensibly a native of Spunkville and a hero of the Aroostook "War," in which he had been wounded when he had tripped on the tongue of a commissary wagon. A group of volunteers waged a mock campaign for Ensign Stebbings, and a number of newspapers throughout the nation publicized the imaginary candidate. The joke, however, offended many members of both major political parties; and, although the satire was discontinued before the election, it nevertheless harmed the magazine.

The fact that the total number of contributors to the *Carpet Bag* during its short lifetime numbered nearly one hundred indicates that Shillaber experienced no difficulty in finding humor to publish. Indeed, the list of contributors includes a number of the most talented contemporary humorists. In addition to Shillaber, the most distinguished contributors were John Townsend Trowbridge, who published stories under the pseudonym Paul Creyton, and Charles G. Halpine, who wrote under several pen names. Other regular contributors were Sylvanus Cobb, Jr. (Enoch Fitz-Whistler); Fred T. Somerby (Cymon); Mathew F. Whittier (Ethan Spike); Tobias H. Miller (Uncle Toby); Moses Kimball (Pedro); Joseph W. Paine (Peregrine); and Benjamin Drew, who wrote under a number of pen names, of which Doctor Digg and Trismegistus were most used. The fact that the magazine also printed apprentice pieces by Mark Twain, Artemus Ward, and John Phoenix—three important members of the next generation of American humorists—shows that the *Carpet Bag* not only provided an opportunity for the younger humorists to publish their work but that it also served as a connecting link between the older and younger nineteenth-century humorists.

Shillaber's own contributions, which were a prominent feature of the magazine, included editorials and light verse. Other attractive features were excellent book reviews, travel sketches, informative articles, and distinctive illustrations by Hammett Billings, G. H. Rouse, D. C. Johnson, and Frank Bellow. Altogether, it was an interesting, attractive, and well-edited magazine with an outstanding corps of writers and illustrators. But despite its generally high quality, the *Carpet Bag* was not a success. Although it was distributed widely over the country, its circulation was limited to only about four hundred copies a week. In October, 1852, Wilder and Pickard attempted to save it by combining it with their *Pathfinder and Railway Guide;* but the effort was not successful, and the last issue appeared on March 26, 1853.

Shillaber himself believed that there were several reasons for its failure: first, it was his opinion that the American people were not yet ready for a magazine devoted exclusively to humor. Second, he was convinced that the political satire in the Ensign Jehiel Stebbings sketches alienated many readers and reduced the circulation of the magazine. Third, he believed that the combined influence of contributors and subscribers altered the original intent of the magazine. In one of the last issues he wrote sorrowfully: "We commenced it with the avowal of our intentions simply to make the genial its characteristic feature—to make it a pleasant companion, merely, rather than a funny one—but for a long time the tide set strongly against us; the impression had gone out that we were of that very funny class that cannot speak without joking—the real 'side-splitting' and 'rib tickling' sort—and in our enterprise was discerned a mine of fun. Men subscribed to it for this reason, contributors wrote for it from the same mistaken idea, and we were compelled, at last, by force of circumstances to make it what it became." [17]

Some thirty-five years later, when reminiscing about the venture, Shillaber wrote: "It was a hazardous innovation, and distrust hardened with every effort made to establish a humorous paper.... The experiment of its publication demonstrated the fact that there was no room in Boston for an exclusively humorous paper...." [18] But, although the *Carpet Bag* survived only two years, it was nevertheless an important publication because it helped to determine the nature and direction of American humor for the next fifty years by serving as an influence on younger humorists, such as Mark Twain and Artemus Ward. It also helped to encourage the publication of native American humor and to give it an air of respectability which it had not previously had. In reference to the influence of the magazine, Shillaber later wrote: "Before the experiment with *The Carpet Bag,* the papers were not prolific of mirth, and the humorous column was not considered essential to journalism, as it became subsequently.... There were humorous writers before *The Carpet Bag,* but the issue of that tended to awaken new effort, or concentrate that which existed." [19]

In 1853 a number of Shillaber's friends financed the publication of *Rhymes With Reason and Without,* his first book. A handsome volume published by Abel Tompkins and B. B. Mussey Company of Boston, the book is a disorganized compilation of verses which had appeared previously in the Boston *Post* and the *Carpet Bag.* Of this book Shillaber later wrote, "The success of the venture was not phenomenal, though the book was not a loss, and its reception by the critics was very kind." [20] He recorded, too, with considerable satisfaction, that both William Cullen Bryant and Oliver Wendell Holmes had praised it.

V *The Boston* Post *Again*

Shortly after the demise of the *Carpet Bag* in March, 1853, Shillaber returned to the Boston *Post* and resumed the position which he had left in 1850. Very soon after his return, however, he was given an opportunity to become a full-fledged newspaperman when the local editor of the *Post* resigned and he was assigned to fill the vacancy. This position he enjoyed immensely since it gave him an opportunity to become more active in business and politics, and in the social and cultural life of Boston. His duties, which were widely varied, included visiting the courts, police stations, sessions of the state legislature and political meetings, and attending lectures, plays, and concerts and reporting on these events. In addition, he assumed again the task of writing "All Sorts of Paragraphs," and he again contributed verse to the columns of the *Post.* He also brought Mrs. Partington back with him and printed numerous sketches featuring her in the columns of the newspaper. Still interested in politics and still a dedicated Democrat, he repeatedly attacked with gusto the Whigs, the Know-Nothings, and the Abolitionists. His enthusiasm for his position on the *Post* was somewhat dampened in 1853, however, when he began to be plagued by attacks of gout, an affliction which tormented and crippled him for the remainder of his life.

Not long after his return to the *Post,* a representative of the publishing firm of J. C. Derby in New York urged Shillaber to prepare a volume of his humor for publication. He immediately went to work on the project, and the book appeared in 1854 under the title *Life and Sayings of Mrs. Partington and Others of the Family.* The book, like the volumes published by most other nineteenth-century humorists, was simply a compilation of pieces which he had published in the *Post* and in the *Carpet Bag;* the book has no discernible organization. A decided success, it sold fifty thousand copies within a few weeks of its publication; it proved to be the best and most popular book which he was to publish. It was with the profits from this book that he bought the house in Chelsea which was his home until his death.

In 1854 with the publication of *Life and Sayings of Mrs. Partington* Shillaber had reached the height of his popularity as a humorist. George W. Bungay, who in 1854 considered him important enough to include in a volume of biographical sketches of the prominent men of the day, described him as follows: "The subject of this sketch is in the prime of life, a stout hale, hearty man, considerable above the common stature, with a plain, frank face, a full breast, an honest heart, and a head clear as crystal. He has dark hair, is of the bilious-nervous temperament, dresses in a careless manner. Since he has become an author, the hole in his coat has disappeared." [21]

In an attempt to capitalize upon his reputation as the creator of Mrs. Partington, Shillaber entered the field of public lecturing as a reader of original verse. He seems to have made his debut as a public lecturer on December 13, 1855, when he presented verses entitled "The Press" before the Mercantile Library Association in Boston. [22] Later in the same season he presented his poem in Manchester, Waltham, South Boston, Winchendon, Newburyport, Clinton, and in several other New England cities. This limited tour seems to have been experimental, and apparently it was not a highly successful venture because there is no evidence that he lectured outside of New England nor that he attempted to lecture again for several years.

VI   *Boston* Saturday Evening Gazette

In 1856 Shillaber relinquished his position on the *Post* to become associate editor of the Boston *Saturday Evening Gazette,* a weekly published by William W. Clapp, Jr. He had become acquainted with Clapp soon after his arrival in Boston in 1833, and over the years they had become close friends. He held this position for ten years, and in it he found the greatest satisfaction of his career as an editor. The *Gazette,* which combined the features of a magazine and newspaper, published fiction, informative articles, and verse as well as news stories; and, since it was the only Sunday newspaper in Boston, it had a large circulation. During Shillaber's very successful years as associate editor, he published a substantial volume of his own verse, comic anecdotes, and humorous, sentimental, and moralistic tales in the *Gazette.* His regular duties seem to have included, too, the writing of two regular columns, one entitled "Melange" and the other "Saturday's Notes." "Melange" was made up of verse, aphorisms, short travel sketches, jokes, humorous anecdotes, and other items of a miscellaneous nature; but "Saturday's Notes" was primarily a summary of the week's news. Mrs. Partington and Ike, of course, immediately became one of the main attractions of the *Gazette;* and Dr. Spooner, Wideswarth, Old Roger, and Blifkins also became prominent features of the paper.

Clapp was an ardent Republican, but the *Gazette* was nonpartisan, although it did strongly support the Union before and during the Civil War. For example, when South Carolina seceded in December, 1860, Shillaber expressed his keen disapproval of the whole movement toward secession in the South. [23] When Fort Sumter was fired upon in April,

1861, he attacked the South for this highly provocative act.[24] In September, 1862, he went so far as to give his hearty approval to the widening of the administration's war aims and President Lincoln's preliminary emancipation proclamation.[25] During the Civil War Shillaber also published in the magazine a number of war poems, several of which he later included in *Lines in Pleasant Places,* a second collection of his poems.

In 1857 Shillaber again entered the field of public lecturing, and for two seasons he was almost constantly on the road lecturing in numerous cities east of the Mississippi River. Like most nineteenth-century lecturers, he found the occupation a demanding, enervating, and lonely one. Railway coaches were drafty and uncomfortable, and hotel rooms were usually cold and dreary. On a railway trip from Wilkes-Barre to New York, the train on which he was riding became snowbound, and he had nothing to eat for an entire day. Concerning one bed in which he slept while on tour, Shillaber wrote:

It was most unquestionably a wire-gauze bed, plump in its seeming but so cold that Dr. Kane at the north pole could not have suffered more than I did. Besides, the sheets were a little damp, and I know there could have been no greater sufferer than myself this side of Siberia. There were different odors about beds,—the oily, the smoky, and the sweet,—the latter not too common,—and the mouldy that had a strange smell of mortality about them, which provoked alarming queries in one's mind as to what use these very sheets might have been put to, and induced dreams of ghouls, and churchyards, and hideous things, that made one wake up shuddering and fancy weights on his eyelids, and shovelfuls of earth upon his heart.[26]

But, in spite of the hardships, he did enjoy seeing the country and the American people. He was perhaps most interested in the many immigrant families moving to the West, particularly in the women, who, he thought, displayed considerable perseverance and competence in managing their possessions, children, and husbands during their journey to new homes on the frontier.

In 1859 he published his third book, entitled *Knitting Work: A Web of Many Textures, Wrought by Ruth Partington.* Published by Brown, Taggard, and Chase, the book is a collection of miscellaneous tales, humorous sketches, and humorous and serious verse culled from the mass of material which he had published in the *Post* and in the *Saturday Evening Gazette* and apparently pieced together with no structural plan in mind. A decided success, the book sold ten thousand copies before publication.[27]

Shillaber found a great deal of satisfaction in his work on the *Gazette,* and he made a considerable contribution to its success, but repeated attacks of gout forced him to remain at home for weeks at a time, and in 1867 he reluctantly gave up his position with the paper. He continued to contribute to it, however, for several years.

VII   *Illness, Poverty, and Death*

During the remaining twenty-three years of his life, Shillaber attempted, not very successfully, to make a living from the publication of books and by selling articles, poems, and stories to magazines and newspapers. He was connected, too, sometime between 1867 and 1871 with *The Flag of Our Banner,* a newspaper published in Boston by Elliott, Thomes, and Talbot.[28] He may also have done some lecturing between 1866 and 1871,[29] and sometime during the 1880's he wrote a weekly column for the Hartford *Post* entitled "Old Man With a Cane." [30] One of the most satisfying experiences of his later years was a trip which he made in 1876 to California.

The most important books which he published during the later years of his life were *Partingtonian Patchwork* (1873), a collection of humorous pieces, and *Lines in Pleasant Places* (1874), a volume of verse which he published at his own expense. He also published three books for boys, the best of which was *Ike Partington; or, The Adventures of a Human Boy and His Friends* (1879).

Because Shillaber possessed, as he put it, "a fatal facility for rhyming," [31] he was overwhelmed with invitations to read occasional verse of his own composition at banquets, festivals, celebrations, commencements, and other public occasions. He worked diligently, too, during the last years of his life on a book of reminiscences of his active years as a writer and journalist in Boston, which he tried hard but unsuccessfully to publish. The work fortunately was published post-humously in serial form in the *New England Magazine* under the title "Experiences During Many Years," and it is an invaluable source of information about Shillaber's life in Boston before about 1870.

The later years of Shillaber's life were not particularly happy ones. Not only did his gout become progressively worse until he was confined to a wheel chair, but he also developed diabetes and heart disease. After his wife's death in 1883, his unmarried daughter Caroline looked after him in his house in Chelsea. To further increase his unhappiness, he was, as he expressed it in a letter, "poor as poverty." [32] Although he continued to publish until almost the end of his life, his humor, popular a generation ago, now had little appeal, and he and Mrs. Partington were almost forgotten. In addition, Shillaber, always a poor business-man, had not capitalized on his earlier success as a shrewder Yankee might have done; and, almost as impractical in many ways as Mrs. Partington, he had little except his house in Chelsea to show for what remuneration he had received for his writing. As a result, he was often forced to ask William W. Clapp, Jr., and other loyal friends for financial assistance.

In a letter written shortly before his death on November 25, 1890, Shillaber summed up his life as follows: "It is no great affair of a life I have given, but I can say, without personal vanity, that during the more than forty years of my connection with the press I have never wittingly encouraged a wrong nor wounded the feelings of a single worthy soul, however he differed from me; always desiring to be counted, like Ben Adhem, as one who loved his fellow men." [33] We feel strongly as we read reminiscences of Benjamin P. Shillaber written by people who knew him personally that the best of him does not appear in his writing. Invariably their accounts stress his wit, his kindliness and generosity, his benevolence and sympathy, his geniality and courtesy, and his cheerfulness in the face of adversity. John Townsend Trowbridge, who knew him well, wrote of him: "I believe it can be said of him more truly than of any man I ever knew . . . that he never made an enemy." [34]

CHAPTER 2

Mrs. Partington

B Y the middle of the nineteenth century two major literary traditions had been established in the United States: the genteel and the vernacular. The genteel tradition, which was endorsed by the literary Establishment and which was still the dominant influence on major writers, involved not only a style of writing but also a philosophy of life. Stylistically, it was strongly inclined toward the formal, the refined, the decorous, and the "literary"; philosophically, it affirmed fixed traditional moral and esthetic values. The vernacular tradition, on the other hand, embraced the use of colloquial language, and it tended to reject conventional values in favor of a pragmatic view of human experience.[1] A popular tradition, it flourished in oral storytelling, popular drama, almanacs, and jest books as well as in newspaper humor.

By the time Shillaber created Mrs. Partington, the vernacular had been used by such writers as Seba Smith, Thomas Chandler Haliburton, Augustus B. Longstreet, and William T. Thompson. Although it had been considered vulgar and subliterary by most educated readers and writers since its inception, it was by Shillaber's time becoming increasingly accepted as a literary idiom; and eventually it helped to effect a radical change in American prose style. Like Mark Twain, Shillaber was always torn between the two traditions; and, also like Twain, he invariably did his best writing when he worked within the confines of the vernacular tradition. It is true that Shillaber produced no work comparable to *Huckleberry Finn,* but he must be given credit for exploring and demonstrating through Mrs. Partington the artistic possiblities of the vernacular and for contributing to its development as a distinctive style of writing. Although he was also strongly attracted to the genteel and published scores of poems, tales, and essays in that mode, his literary reputation today rests entirely upon his creation of one character—Mrs. Partington.

I *Her Humor*

Before Shillaber created Mrs. Partington, he had experimented briefly with several comic characters in his column in the Boston *Post,* but all of them were artistic failures. His successful creation in 1847 of Mrs. Partington was more the result of accident than of careful and deliberate design. Concerning the genesis of Mrs. Partington, he later wrote:

Down to 1847 I had been a manipulator of the stick and rule, with no ambitious aspirations for a literary career, content to leave the acquisition of fame, by writing, to those who desired it, and beyond a few ordinary squibs in the "All Sorts of Paragraphs," had not committed myself to paper, when a simple accident, like many which influence human events of greater import than that I am about to describe, set a "ball rolling" which has scarcely ceased its revolution at this later day. "Paregorically speaking" I draw my garments aside, and shake my shoes from my feet as I enter the charmed circle wherein sits enshrined the mythical being before whom, Pygmalion-like, I offered incense in days whilom. To me she became life, and went with me to make me see queer things and say queer things under her inspiration: her antique bonnet, her "ridicule" and specs winning way to many firesides and introducing her chronicler to a fame undreamt of. . . . There was no thought beyond that passing moment, no dream of subsequent effort, not the most remote idea of future fame; but the time was favorable for something of the kind, the ambition of a first success was excited, more was called for, and soon that which was so singularly and unpretendingly begun became a necessity of the author, grew famous in a small way and attained voluminous proportions.[2]

Since the early pieces are not presented dramatically and since Mrs. Partington is little more than a name, the humor does not grow out of her language, actions, or personality. The following squib, which appeared in the *Post* on June 15, 1847, is typical of Shillaber's earliest efforts: "Mrs. Partington attended the launch of the Ocean Monarch on Saturday, and the old lady told us, with tears in her eyes, that, after wasting an hour and a half, she merely stooped down to tie her shoe, when the ship run off, and she didn't see the sight after all."

Within a short time, however, Shillaber learned to allow his character to speak for herself in the vernacular, and his sketches generally took the form of short monologues. This stage in the development of his presentation of Mrs. Partington is clearly seen in the following piece, which appeared in the *Post* on July 10, 1847: " 'Isn't there some claws in the revised statutes against cats,' said Mrs. Partington; 'it seems to me there ought to be, for my poor Paul once got terribly torn in his flesh and trowsers by one, and for nothing at all either, but just sitting down on her—and the cloth cost a dollar a yard, too.' "

As time went on, Shillaber extended and refined his delineation of Mrs. Partington with characteristic action and patterns of thought. Introducing secondary characters and dialogue into the Partington pieces, he also lengthened them and cast them in the form of the anecdote. The following anecdote in the August 11, 1847, issue of the *Post* illustrates this third stage in the evolution of Shillaber's art: " 'How do you like the bustle and confusion of Boston? ' asked the shopkeeper, as Mrs. Partington stood by the counter. 'It gives me confusion to see 'em,' said the old lady; 'folks didn't do so when I was a girl; and besides, what an awful lot of bran and cotton it takes, to say nothing of their awkwardness when they get slipped to one side—' 'I mean,' broke in the shopkeeper, 'the bustle and confusion of the streets.' 'Oh!' said Mrs. P., 'that is quite *another thing*!' and immediately left the store." In subsequent anecdotes, Shillaber extended the action, lengthened the dialogue, created Ike, introduced other secondary characters, and provided more detailed settings. And, more important, he explored in considerably more depth the character of Mrs. Partington.

Although the numerous Partington pieces present the story of the comic heroine's life in a fragmented or disjointed fashion, we can piece together the pattern of her fictitious existence from them and from a brief burlesque biography which Shillaber wrote for *Life and Sayings of Mrs. Partington.*[3] Descended from the Puritans, she was born Ruth Trotter in Dog's Bondage some time before 1800. Upon marrying Paul Partington in 1808, she went to live with him in the small rural village of Beanville, located somewhere in Massachusetts. Although Paul was hardly the military hero which Mrs. Partington later imagined he had been, he did serve as a corporal in the War of 1812. The couple had no children, but after Paul's death, she willingly took Paul's nephew Ike Partington to rear. When the Partington home was razed to make way for the Beanville Railroad, she and Ike moved to Boston, fortress of the genteel tradition. There, among the Brahmins, the two unlettered provincials attend plays, lectures, concerts, the opera, and other cultural events with no feeling of inferiority whatsoever.

Shillaber's treatment of his two innocents and their unsophisticated reactions to the cultural life of Boston reveals clearly the basic conflict in him between the allurement of the genteel and the attraction of the vernacular. Like Mark Twain in *Innocents Abroad,* Shillaber is drawn first toward one tradition and then toward the other. Sometimes he sympathizes with the inability of his vernacular characters to come to grips with the established culture; at other times he laughs gently at them because they have no real understanding of it nor genuine appreciation for it. At still other times he is ambivalent and does not reveal to the reader where his sympathies lie.

In creating Mrs. Partington, Shillaber relied heavily upon his memories of his boyhood and young manhood in New Hampshire. Although he was well acquainted with R. B. Thomas's *Old Farmer's Almanac,* George Handel ("Yankee") Hill, the actor, and the numerous Yankee plays, Seba Smith's Jack Downing, Thomas Chandler Haliburton's Sam Slick, and indeed the whole tradition of Yankee humor, he drew Mrs. Partington primarily from his firsthand knowledge of Yankee life, speech, and character. In his preface to *Life and Sayings of Mrs. Partington* he wrote, "The character has been drawn from life. The Mrs. Partington we have depicted is no fancy sketch, and no malaprop imitation, as some have thought who saw in it naught but distorted words and queer sentences. We need no appeal to establish this fact. Mrs. Partington is seen everywhere, and as often without the specs and cap as with them." [4] Of stage Yankees he said, "The majority of Yankee comedians bear the same resemblance to the New Englander of everyday life that the profiles in black of itinerant cutters bear to the faces of those they are intended to represent." [5]

Although Ruth Partington is feminine rather than masculine, she has the salient characteristics of the crackerbox oracles who preceded and followed her: she is of rural origin; she is representative of the common people; and she plays the role of the wise fool. Characteristically Yankee, her humor lies in her style, her comic monologues, her understatement, and her epigrams. Unlike most of the heroes of Yankee humor, however, she is never sly or devious; and she is not a schemer. She is uneducated, practical, direct, literal-minded, amiable, humane, naïve, and garrulous; her distinctive trait is her benevolence, not her sagacity. Her characteristic vices are her use of snuff, her addiction to tea, and her employment of malapropisms. Her chief interests lie in animals, religion, home remedies, current events, gardening, and conversation. Although she can be very tactless, she is all heart. Her wise aphorisms are usually accidents; when she consciously attempts to be oracular, as she often does, she is comically platitudinous. Because she has no inhibitions about giving advice or about talking to anyone on any subject at any time, Shillaber's choice of subject matter for his humor is almost unlimited.

Shillaber was annoyed by the fact that many contemporary readers and critics did not comprehend the true character of Mrs. Partington, and he felt compelled several times to defend and explain his creation. The most common misconception was that she was merely a pale copy of Mrs. Malaprop and that the only humor in the sketches lay in her misuse of words and was therefore superficial. In a letter to E. S. Marsh, Shillaber wrote, "Mrs. Malaprop I conceive to be quite a different character. When her words are miscalled they come as a part of dialogue, whereas Mrs. P.'s *profound* sayings form pictures in themselves, the framework is auxiliary, giving them piquancy." [6]

When *Graham's Magazine* spoke of Mrs. Partington as an imitation of Mrs. Malaprop, Shillaber wrote in the *Carpet Bag* as follows:

Mrs. Partington ("of ours! ") is as different from Mrs. Malaprop as chalk is from cheese, as we understand the characters. It may be a trifle to speak about, but Mrs. Partington is to us what Mr. Graham's magazine is to Mr. Graham, and as for the imitation we can see none, save where nature has been imitated, which imitation we must confess to, at times, for there is hardly a hamlet or home that has not its Mrs. Partington—some kind old relic of a past age, when educational facilities were not as good as in our own day—whose benevolence and good intention have gone far beyond her grammar, and whose mistakes of the tongue are more than made up by the bountiful love of her heart. We have been complimented much for the truthfulness of this character and confess to a little pique, on seeing the myth of our own raising denounced as a *"plagiarist."* The name was borrowed, alone; it was for us to give the name a locality and a character, and have been assured that we have succeeded. [7]

In commenting on the numerous imitations of Mrs. Partington which appeared in print after his initial success with her in the *Post,* Shillaber wrote in "Experiences During Many Years": "They almost universally misrepresented the character of the amiable old dame, seeing in her sayings nothing beyond the misapplication of words, and often putting into her mouth utterances at which her chaste spirit could but blush. I felt, as I read them, like the old sexton in Salem, who had rung the church bell for thirty years, and when he removed to Marblehead, said that every time he heard that bell, he knew that he was not ringing it. The critics of Mrs. Partington have made the same mistake." [8]

Unlike many other contemporary humorists, Shillaber does not assume the point of view of his character. Although Mrs. Partington usually expresses Shillaber's own ideas and attitudes, she does not function as his alter ego. In contrast to the humorists of the old Southwest, Shillaber does not cast his humor in the form of the leisurely and digressive tale. The Mrs. Partington sketches are anecdotes written from a third-person point of view. The narrator may or may not comment upon the speech or action in his own voice; and, when he does, his more formal style often clashes comically with the vernacular spoken by Mrs. Partington. The best of the anecdotes are short and economical and are characterized by a minimum of authorial intrusion.

The most successful of the anecdotes tend to follow the same simple but effective three-part structural design. The first, or introductory part, opens with a statement or exclamation by Mrs. Partington directed to Ike, Old Roger, Dr. Spooner, a shopkeeper, a bus driver, the narrator, or to no one in particular. Following this introduction, the narrator briefly clarifies for the reader the frame of reference for Mrs. Partington's comment. The second part of the anecdote consists of a monologue by Mrs. Partington or a dialogue between her and the narrator, or another character, in which she enlarges upon her opening remark. During the course of this monologue or dialogue, in which her blunders in the use of words usually result in a malapropism or two, she often manages in her confused way to express a bit of homely wisdom; and the action is usually quite limited. The third part, or the conclusion, of the anecdotes, displays considerable variety. As a result of awkwardness or vehemence Mrs. Partington may knock something over, Ike may do something mischievous, or the narrator may conclude the narrative with a brief comment.

The following anecdote, entitled "Appointing Inspectors," illustrates well the typical structural pattern of Shillaber's more successful anecdotes:

"Inspector of customs! " said Mrs. Partington, as she laid down the paper chronicling some new appointment. Here was a new idea, that broke upon her mind like a ray of sunshine through a corn barn.

"Inspector of customs! " and she looked up at the rigid profile of the old Corporal, as if she would ask what he had to say about it; but that warrior had hung there too long to be now disturbed by trifles, and he took no notice of her.

"Inspector of customs! " continued she, as she turned her attention to the old black teapot, and then turned out the tea, which celestial beverage gurgled through the spout, in harmony with her reflections, not too strong; "that's a new idea to me. But, thank Providence, I ha'nt got no customs that I hadn't as lives they'd inspect as not; only I'd a little rather they wouldn't. I wish everybody could say so, but I'm afeard there are many customs that won't bear looking into. Well, let every tub stand on its own bottom, I say—I won't cast no speciousness on nobody. But I don't see what they wanted to appoint any more for, and be to so much suspense when every place has so many in it that will inspect customs for nothing. If they'd only make my next-door neighbor, Miss Juniper, now, an inspector of customs, they wouldn't need another for a long ways, that's mortally sartin."

She stirred her souchong as she ruminated, untasting, and Ike helped himself, unheeded, to the last preserved pear there was in the dish.[9]

Much of the humor of the anecdotes is inherent in Mrs. Partington's language, which is meant to represent a lower-class New England dialect and to typify the speech of the American "democrat" of the mid-nineteenth century. Her style, which is distinguished by regional expressions, jumbled syntax, and unconventional grammar, has the unmistakable sound of speech. In contrast to many later humorists like Artemus Ward and Josh Billings, Shillaber used misspelling only to indicate phonetically the dialect she spoke and never as a mere comic device. Spellings like "nuther" for "neither," "arter" for "after," "ile" for "oil," "airth" for "earth," "pint" for "point," and "gin" for "give" are attempts to render her pronunciation of these words. Such usages as "hain't" for "haven't," "ain't" for "isn't," and "knowed" for "knew" are also characteristic of her dialect, as is her frequent use of double negatives. Since Shillaber does not overdo his rendition of the dialect, the style does not get in the way of the reader's understanding nor blunt the effect of the humor as it often does, for example, in the Sut Lovingood tales of George Washington Harris.

Of the various verbal techniques which Shillaber employed in his humor, the most common is undoubtedly malapropism. Contemporary critics complained that he used the device excessively, and their objections were probably justified. When a single sketch is stuffed with malapropisms, the humorous effect is certainly blunted:

"Diseases is very various," said Mrs. Partington, as she returned from a street-door conversation with Dr. Bolus. "The Doctor tells me that poor old Mrs. Haze has got two buckles on her lungs! It is dreadful to think of, I declare. The diseases is *so* various! One way we hear of people's dying of hermitage of the lungs; another way of the brown creatures; here they tell us of the elementary canal being out of order, and there about tonsors of the throat; here we hear of neurology in the head, there of an embargo; one side of us we hear of men being killed by getting a pound of tough beef in the sarcofagus, and there another kills himself by discovering his jocular vein. Things change so, that I declare I don't know how to subscribe for any disease now-a-days. New names and new nostrils takes the place of the old, and I might as well throw my old herb-bag away."

Fifteen minutes afterwards Isaac had that herb-bag for a target, and broke three squares of glass in the cellar window in trying to hit it, before the old lady knew what he was about. She didn't mean exactly what she said.[10]

But, since Mrs. Partington is unlettered and her vocabulary limited, her use of an occasional malapropism can be both believable and funny:

"Adulterated tea! " said Mrs. Partington, as she read in the Transcript an account of the adulteration of teas in England, at which she was much shocked. "I wonder if this is adulterated? " and she bowed her head over the steaming and fragrant decoction in the cup before her, whose genial odors mingled with the silvery vapor, and encircled her venerable poll like a halo. "It smells virtuous," continued she, smiling with satisfcation, "and I know this Shoo-shon tea must be good, because I bought it of Mr. Shoo-shon himself, at Redding's. Adulterated! " she meandered on, pensively as a brook in June, "and it's agin the commandment, too, which says—don't break that, Isaac!" as she saw that interesting juvenile amusing himself with making refracted sunbeams dance upon the wall, and around the dark profile, and among the leaves of the sweet fern, like yellow butterflies or fugitive chips of new June butter. The alarm for her crockery dispelled all disquietude about the tea, and she sipped her beverage, all oblivious of dele-tea-rious infusions.[11]

Of the other verbal devices which Shillaber frequently employed, one of the most effective, if not the most original, was that of exploiting the dissimilarity between the genteel and the vernacular by juxtaposing Mrs. Partington's language and the highly artificial style of another speaker. The resulting incongruity is effective and humorous: "Said Augustus as he gazed down from Mrs. Partington's little window, his finger resting upon a cracked china teapot upon the sill—'Here is a spot in which to cultivate the flowers of poesy; here the imagination may soar on unrestricted wing; here balmy zephyrs rising from embowering roses waft ambrosial sweets'—'Them is beans planted in the window,' said the old lady interrupting him. . . ." [12]

In some of the anecdotes the humor results not only from the mixture of the genteel and the vernacular but also from Mrs. Partington's inability to grasp the meaning of a more elevated and opulent variety of English than the one she employs:

"Does Isaac manifest any taste for poetry, Mrs. Partington? " asked the schoolmaster's wife, while conversing on the merits of the youthful Partington. The old lady was basting a chicken that her friends had sent her from the country.

"O, yes! " said the old lady, smiling; "he is very partially fond of poultry, and it always seems as if he can't get enough of it." The old spit turned by the fire-place in response to her answer while the basting was going on.

"I mean," said the lady, "does he show any of the divine afflatus? "

The old lady thought a moment. "As for the divine flatness—I don't know about it. He's had all the complaints of children, and when he was a baby he fell and broke the cartridge of his nose; but I hardly think he's had this that you speak of."

The roasting chicken hissed and sputtered, and Mrs. Partington basted it again. [13]

Again Mrs. Partington's insecure grasp of the spoken language and her consequent mispronunciation of words often lead to comic confusion:

"Have you seena? " asked Mrs. Partington of the apothecary.

"Seen whom? " said he, smiling, as he recognized the dame.

"Why, seena, to be sure," emphasizing the word, "Seena!"

"I have not, my dear madam, the least idea of whom you are inquiring, but I have seen no one whose presence has given me greater pleasure than your own."

"Well, certainly," she said, "that's very kind of you, but I want to know if you have *seena*? "

"Madam, I assure you," replied he, despairingly, "that I do not know what you mean. I have seen hundreds, thousands, multitudes, but have not seen *her,* among them all, that I know of."

"But you have manners? " said she; "and they go together."

"*What,* in Heaven's name? " he almost shrieked, startling the old lady into looking at him anxiously through her "parabolical" spectacles, and drawing Ike away from an attempt to carom three soap-balls on the counter, to the great amusement of the cat.

"Why, seena and manners," replied she calmly, "for a gentle purgatory."

"Oh, senna and manna! " he repeated *sotto voce,* and procured it for her. She went out as gracefully as a seventy-four, and soon was hull down in the distance.[14]

Or the humor may arise from her lapses into syllepsis, her fastening upon the wrong meaning of a common word which has several possible denotations:

Mrs. Partington has a vague idea concerning the statute laws—they are with her things, living, moving, acting—possessing a superior agency in the affairs of life coeval with life itself, and fully as important in their operation as the fundamental laws that control human existence. What was her horror one day to read in the paper a paragraph on the better execution of the laws. She was always anti-capital punishment, because hanging didn't do nobody no good that was hanged. "Execute the Laws! " cried she, "Why, that is inhumanity to brutes; what do they want to execute the poor things for? They wouldn't do anybody no harm if they would let 'em alone. It is the plaguy lawyers and constables and sich that ought to be executed, I think." With what energy was this delivered, and there was a graceful dignity too in the complete wave of her hand that knocked the coffee-pot off the table.[15]

Sometimes she attempts to ape literary language by using figures of speech. These attempts usually end comically in complete disaster. For example, in discussing changing fashions in women's dresses, she says, "Well, for my part I don't see what they want to make a public thing of it for; changing the dress used to be a private matter; but folks do so alter! They are always a changing dresses now, like the caterpillar in the morning that turns into a butterfly at night, or the butterfly that turns into a caterpillar in the morning, I don't know which." [16]

The following anecdote achieves its comic effect both from Mrs.

Partington's proclivity to use malapropisms and her valiant attempt to use figurative language:

Mrs. Partington attended the dedication of Mount Hope Cemetery, in Dorchester, and got wet with the rain. No sheltering umbrella was there to hold its broad surface above her venerable head; and the rain, all regardless of her august presence, poured down relentlessly. But we will let her tell the story in her own way.

"The seminary would have been dictated, but, by an imposition of divine Providence, the bottles of heaven were uncorked and the rains fell as if another delusion was agoing to destroy the world. The lightning blazed horridly, and everybody was filled with constipation. Not a shelter to be had! I tried to lean over and get my bonnet under a gentleman's umbrel, in front of me, and the water all run down into my back like a spout, till I was satiated through and through like an old boot. Cold chills run over me as if I had an ager, and, O dear! look at that bonnet."

Certainly the faded remnant had wilted, the pasteboard that formed the crown had relaxed and shook flabbily as we held it, and irreparable decay seemed written upon it.

"It never will be fit to be seen again! " said she, and we fancied a tone of deeper sorrow in her words, as she looked straight up at the stiff old corporal on the wall, whom this antique crape commemorated. Heaven bless thee, Mrs. Partington! we thought, and felt round our capacious pocket for a dollar to leave with her, but, as it usually happens when our benevolence comes on, we found none, and came away with a paper pinned to our coat-tail by that "everlasting Ike." [17]

All of the humor in the Mrs. Partington sketches, however, does not lie merely in the unconventional nature of the language itself; for the language reveals character, and much of the fun is inherent in the erratic thought processes and the peculiar quality of the undisciplined mind of the old lady herself. Frequently the humor is found in logical absurdities which are the result of her muddled thinking. In one of the earlier pieces, for example, we find: " 'Those must be some of them foreign relations of ours,' said Mrs. Partington on seeing a wagon load of emigrants pass her door, 'they seem very poor, though; but they shouldn't be despised and ill treated for that, for we may be *born* poor ourselves yet,'—and the old lady smiled mildly and wished a blessing on them as they passed." [18] In another monologue she says, "A dozen children may seem a large family with our folks, who are moderates, but my poor dear husband used to tell the story of a woman in some part of the world where he stopped one night, who had nineteen children in five years; or five children in nineteen years, I don't recollect which; but I remember it was one or t'other."[19]

Sometimes illogical thinking is combined with anticlimax. For example, in one of the sketches, after Ike has used profanity, she says, "Stop, Isaac, and don't never let me hear you say sich a word again; it's agin scriptur and natur and everything. Why you never even hear the brute beasts swear, and how dreadful it is that a man should, or a nice little boy, that can think and speak." [20]

In other sketches she may, on the other hand, play the role of the wise fool and come up with an astute and amusing observation in spite of her unreliable intellect:

"So you've come down to attend the adversary meetings," said Mrs. Partington, as she surveyed the three trunks and two valises and a basket that the cab had just left, and the owner of them all, a gentleman in black, with a ghostly-looking neckcloth.

"Ah! " said he, humoring her conceit and smiling for he expected to stay some days, "the adversary *we* meet we subdue with the weapons of the spirit."

"That is just what dear Deacon Sprig said when he captivated the crazy Ingen with New England rum and then put him in bride'll. Says he, 'I'll subdue him with the sword of the spirit'—he was a sich a queer man. Those meetings are excellent for converting heathens and saving the lost, and I do hope, after they have saved everybody else, that they will try and save a few more of their own that need teaching. There are a great many round here that want looking after more than the heathen do; and we must look after our own first, or be worse than the infiddles." [21]

When Mrs. Partington consciously tries to be oracular, as she often does, she usually utters platitudes or belabors self-evident truths in a comical manner:

"I've always noticed," said Mrs. Partington on New Year's Day, dropping her voice to the key that people adopt when they are disposed to be philosophical or moral; "I've always noticed that every year added to a man's life is apt to make him older, just as a man who goes a journey finds, as he jogs on, that every mile he goes brings him nearer where he is going, and farther from where he started. I am not so young as I was once, and I don't believe I ever shall be, if I live to the age of Samson, which, Heaven knows as well as I do, I don't want to, for I wouldn't be a centurian or an octagon, and survive my factories, and become idiomatic, by any means. But then there is no way of knowing how a thing will turn out till it takes place; and we shall come to an end someday, though we may never live to see it." [22]

In her frequent and earnest efforts to impart some of her large store of wisdom to Ike, her disorderly thought processes and jumbled syntax usually result in incoherence and comic confusion:

"Never get in debt, Isaac," said Mrs. Partington; and she raised her tea-spoon with an oracular air, and held it thus, as if from it were suspended the threads of a fine argument on economy, discernible to her eye alone, and she was watching an opportunity to make it tangible. "Never get in debt, no matter whether you are creditable or not; it is better to live on a crust of bread and water and a herring or two, than cows and oxen cut up into rump steaks, and owe for it. Think of our neighbor; what a failing he had, and had all his goods and impertinences took away on a mean procession and sold, and his poor wife reduced to a calico gound, starvation, and shushon tea, and he in Californy! "

"Some tea, please," said Ike, as he handed over his tin dipper. The tea, like her own reflections, trickled out musically; and she passed along the caution, with the cream and sugar, never to get in debt. [23]

Sometimes the humor turns on Mrs. Partington's simplicity and naïveté. The humor in the following piece arises from the fact that, not understanding the nature of drama, she confuses art with real life:

"The play-house is the *'way to the pit!* ' " said Mrs. Partington, solemnly, and pointing significantly downward.

"But," remonstrated a friend, who had asked her to visit the Museum with him, "there is no pit in this theatre, and the *way* to the pit is removed."

She looked earnestly at him a moment, and then said she would go. The play was the "Stranger," and she was much interested in it.

"Why don't he make it up with her? " she inquired. "What's the sense of being ugly when she's so contricious for what she had done, I should like to know? I think it shows a bad temper in him; and the dear children, too, coming in like little cherubs, to make 'em forget all old troubles and follies! We hadn't ought to dwell so upon old grievousness, because we are all liable creatures. How I do pity her! "

And the old lady wept copiously. She wouldn't leave the house till she ascertained from the policeman whether old Tobias got back his son that had 'listed, for he looked but feeble, she said, when he went away, and the great grief and the long pole the old gentleman carried for a cane must have broken him down.[24]

Ballet is equally incomprehensible to her:

"When is the bally troop coming on? " said Mrs. Partington, after watching the dancers at the Boston Theatre about half an hour.—"That is the ballet troupe," said Augustus, with a smile, pointing at the beautiful sylphs that were fluttering like butterflies about the stage. She looked at him incredulously for a little while, and said: "Well, I believe in calling things by their true names; and what they call them a troop for, I don't see. I thought it was a troop of horses, such as they had in the Contract of the Ganges." She levelled her new opera glass at the stage, and looked long and earnestly. "Well," said she, "if there ever was anybody that needed sympathy, it's them! Worn their dresses way up to their knees by dancing, poor creaturs! and by and by, at this rate, they won't have nothing to wear." She stood beating time as the waves of gauze moved hither and thither in illustration of the poetry of motion, while Ike amused himself by tearing up his theatre-bill, and putting it into a lady's silk hood, which hung over the back of the front seat.[25]

In several of Mrs. Partington's monologues, the fun lies in the fact that, somewhat like Jim Blaine in Mark Twain's "The Story of the Old Ram," the old lady lets her mind be led astray by a chain of association which finally leads to nothing at all: " 'I wonder what family of Smiths "John Smith, Jr.," who writes for the Post, belongs to? ' said Mrs. Partington. 'He must, I think be the son of old Consideration Smith, that lived in our neighborhood in the last war; and this John must be the one who they said had a sneaking notion after sister Lucy—an awful homely man he was too, I remember; but come to think of it, his father's name wasn't Smith, but Switchell, and John's name, I believe, was Joshua.' "[26]

Since Shillaber's best humor invariably grows directly out of the firmly conceived character of Mrs. Partington and not out of verbal pyrotechnics, it is genuinely artistic rather than shallow and superficial.

Even her boundless benevolence, which is the very hallmark of her
virtue, can lead to humor, as it does in the following:

Before Ike dropped the cat, it was a matter of much annoyance to
Mrs. Partington, upon coming down stairs one morning, to find a litter
of kittens in her Indian work-basket, beside her black Sunday bonnet
and upon the black gloves and handkerchief, long consecrate to grief.
Ike had left the basket uncovered, during a search for some thread to
make a snare to catch a pigeon with. Her temper was stirred by the
circumstance, as what good, tidy housekeeper's would not have been by
such an occurrence?

"I'll drownd 'em," said she, "every one of 'em! O, you wicked
creatur! " continued she, raising her finger, and shaking it at the cat;
"O, you wicked creatur, to serve me such a trick! "

But the cat, happy in the joys of maternity, purred gladly among her
offspring, and looked upon the old lady, through her half-closed eyes,
as if she didn't really see any cause for such a fuss.

"Isaac," said the dame, "take the big tub, and drownd them
kittens."

There was determination in her eye, and authority in her tone, and
Ike clapped his hands as he hastened to obey her.

"Stop, Isaac, a minute," she cried, "and I'll take the chill off the
water; it would be cruel to put 'em into it stone-cold."

She took the steaming kettle from the stove, and emptied it into the
tub, and then left the rest to Ike. But she reproached herself for her
inhumanity long afterwards, and could not bear to look the childless
cat in the face, and many a dainty bit did that injured animal receive
from her mistress. Mrs. Partington perhaps did wrong, as who hasn't at
some period of life? Perfection belongeth not to man or woman, and
we would throw this good pen of ours into the street, and never take
another in our fingers, could we pretend that Mrs. Partington was an
exception to this universal rule.[27]

II *Her Satire*

Although Shillaber was basically a humorist rather than a satirist, a
slender but clearly discernible thread of satire runs through the Mrs.
Partington sketches. Always gentle and good-natured rather than harsh
and vindictive, he generally employs humor rather than invective as the
vehicle of his criticism. Of corrosive satire, he wrote: "Satire is an ugly
weapon in the work of reform. It tears asunder, it cauterizes, it blisters.

No one is really made better through it. The assailed, though he may fear the sting, will never be better through its application, though he may *seem* so. A satirist lives all the time in boiling water." [28]

Despite Shillaber's consuming interest in politics, he seldom used Mrs. Partington as a weapon in his attacks on the Whigs or in his debates on the vital issues of the day. Generally, he confined himself to poking fun at the weaknesses of human nature, particularly greed and hypocrisy, and at extremists of all kinds. Although Shillaber could not be called a reformer, his satire indicates that he wished people were better, less selfish, kinder, and more honest in all things. His satiric norm was disinterested benevolence, and his code of ethics was that subscribed to, in theory if not in practice, by most of his contemporaries.

Although Shillaber was a strong democrat and believed at least theoretically in the goodness and wisdom of the common man, his view of human nature was realistic rather than sentimental; and he was not blind to the many defects of human nature. He was convinced, for example, that, although benevolence is a prime virtue, it is futile to expect that kindness will be rewarded with gratitude. When, for example, a dog which Mrs. Partington has rescued from a pond splashes muddy water all over her dress, she says, "he couldn't have been more ungrateful if he had been a human critter." [29] Again when a neighbor neglects to replace some eggs she has borrowed, Mrs. Partington says, "When I lent her the eggs . . . she said she would be eternally indebted to me, and I guess she will. How can people do so?" [30] The avariciousness of people also disturbed Shillaber. When New Englanders were hurrying by the thousands to California in 1849 during the gold rush, the following monologue by Mrs. Partington appeared in the *Post:*

"Dear me!" exclaimed Mrs. Partington sorrowfully, "how much a man will bear, and how far he will go, to get this soddered dross, as Parson Martin called it when he refused the beggar a sixpence for fear it might lead him into extravagance; everybody is going to California and chargin arter gold. Cousin Jones and three Smiths have gone; and Mr. Chip the carpenter has left his wife and seven children and blessed old mother-in-law to seek his fortin tu. This is the strangest yet, and I don't see how he could have done it; it looks so ungrateful to treat heaven's blessings so lightly. But then, we are told that the love of money is the root of all evil, and how true it is, for they are still rooting arter it like pigs arter ground nuts. Why it is a perfect moneymania among everybody;" and she shook her head doubtingly as she pensively watched a small mug of cider with an apple in it simmering by the winter fire; she was somewhat fond of drink made in this way.[31]

The Mrs. Partington sketches contain some evidence, too, that, despite Shillaber's strong democratic leanings, he had some serious doubts about the ability of the common people to govern themselves. In the sketch "Torchlight Patriotism," Mrs. Partington says over the noise made by what Shillaber calls ironically "the unterrified democracy" in a torchlight procession, "I do love to see the unclarified democracy in possession, with their torches a blazing and their patrickism a busting."[32]

He was not, on the other hand, above poking fun at the Boston Brahmins and the pretensions of their genteel culture. Often he sympathizes with Mrs. Partington's bewilderment and confusion at concerts, the opera, lyceum, lectures, and ballet. In one of his more amusing anecdotes he chides Ralph Waldo Emerson, certainly one of the most illustrious of the Brahmins, for the complexity and abstractness of his public lectures. Although Shillaber's attitude in the anecdote is ambiguous, he certainly suggests strongly that Mrs. Partington's difficulty in comprehending Emerson's lecture is not altogether the result of her own obtuseness:

The venerable Mrs. Partington asked us the question, once, if we believed that everything was foreördained beforehand in advance, and we were compelled to answer that sometimes we did, and then again we didn't. Some time after, we were sitting looking over the papers, when the door opened and Mrs. P. stepped in. There was a smile on her face, and the old green umbrella in her hand. After welcoming her and requesting her to be seated, she said, "Well it's all lubricated now; just as clear to me as crystial."—"What is? " we queried, a little puzzled to know what she meant—"That about foreördination, you know, and chance, and all that, which we were talking about."—"Ah, yes; well, how was it?"—"Why, I 'tended the lectur' last night—one of the eternity course."—"Fraternity,"we suggested; "who spoke? "—"O, Mr. what's his name—he that made the refrigerator, you know, for warming houses in summer and cooling 'em in winter—Emerson—T. P. Emerson."—"You mean R. W. Emerson," we hinted; "did he lecture on refrigerators?"—"O, dear, no 't was on chance; and sich a lectur'! I thought I'd heerd lecturs before, but that succeeded 'em all."—"Indeed! " we said, somewhat interested, though there were eleven letters unopened on the table, "tell us about it."—"Well," she continued, "it was about chance, and he is such a queer man that you have to watch every word or you can't understand him. If you lose one word, it's jest like a stitch broke in a seam made by some of the sowing-machines—the work is good for nothing. Well, he said there was no such thing as chance, and that everything was planned out beforehand. And, to prove it, he spoke of a ship on the sea, knocked about by the winds and waves, and showed, just as loosed as anything I ever saw, that she was not there by chance, or that she was, and I declare I don't know which." The old lady reached down into her spacious pocket, and, taking out the old Constitution and Guerrière handkerchief, wiped her specs, as though she wished still for more light while Ike amused himself trundling Lion round the room, by his two hind legs, like a wheelbarrow. [33]

Shillaber had the temerity, too, to make sport of Harvard University, one of the fountainheads of the genteel. When, for example, someone, in discussing the Crimean War, mentions the "Turkish question" to Mrs. Partington, she says, "For gracious sake ain't there nobody to answer it? Why don't they get the Harvard Universalists to answer it, for they have a great faculty over there to Cambridge among the professors; though arter all I never see much difference between professors and other folks in pint of knowingness, nor goodness neither for that matter." [34]

Because of her ignorance and her naïveté Mrs. Partington is completely taken in by some of the bizarre forms which the genteel assumed. When, for example, she is asked in one of the sketches if her husband was obese, she tries valiantly to imitate the artificial language of an elocutionist whom she had heard the previous night; and she grandiloquently answers, "A beast, indeed! look at that," and she pointed to the rigid portrait on the wall. "See if you can find anything beastly in them liniments, where Job himself did set his sealing wax to give the world insurance of a man." [35] In another sketch, she is completely captivated by the elegant language, the artificial gestures, and the commanding stage presence of a young elocutionist:

"O, doesn't he disclaim fluidly! " exclaimed Mrs. Partington, delightedly, as she listened to the exercises of the Humtown Intellectual Mutual Improvement Society. Her admiration knew no bounds as a young declaimer, with inspiration truly Demosthenic, launched the flashing beams of his eloquence broadcast among his auditors, with thrilling, dazzling, burning force; anon soaring like a rocket into the "empyrean blue," dashing helter skelter amidst the stars, and harnessing the fiery comets to the car of his genius; anon scouring the land like a racer, the hot sparks, like young lightning marking his Phaetonish course; anon breaking through the terraqueous shell, and revelling in Hadean horrors in underground localities somewhere.

The voice of Mrs. Partington, whom we left standing on the threshold of her admiration some way back, recalls us to herself.

"How fluidly he talks! He ought to be a minister, I declare; and how well he would look with a surplus on, to be sure! He stands on the nostrum as if he was born and bred an oratorio all his life. I wish the President was here to-night; I know he'd see he was an extr'ord'nary young man, and like as not appint him minister extr'ord'nary, instead of some that never preached any at all."

The old lady beat time with her fan to his gesticulations, nodding the black bonnet approvingly, and smiled as the young man told the world that Franklin had made it a present of the printing-press.[36]

In both anecdotes Shillaber is, of course, poking fun at Mrs. Partington for being taken in, but he is also clearly expressing his amusement at the conventions of nineteenth-century oratory.

In several of the Mrs. Partington anecdotes, Shillaber, who was not particularly fond of opera, gently satirizes the current popularity of Italian opera. No doubt many Americans who flocked to operas got little more satisfaction from them than does Mrs. Partington in the following anecdote:

"I can't catch the malady! " said Mrs. Partington at the opera, as she stood on tiptoe, in the lobby of the Howard Athenaeum, in vain attempting to look over the heads before her. She had received a ticket, but it secured nothing but an outside position, and she had gone wandering round like a jolly planet, without any particular orbit. Ike was in the gallery, eating a penny's worth of pea-nuts and throwing the shells into the parquet below. "I can't catch the malady of the uproar, and more in half the words are all Dutch to me. This is the first opiatic performance I ever went to, and if I can't find a seat, I can't stand it to come agin." [37]

Other objects of Shillaber's satire were the reform movements and religious cults which were so prominent a feature of mid-nineteenth-century American culture. Although Shillaber is never abusive in his treatment of the reformers and cultists, he obviously has little sympathy for their causes and much less for their ardor in promoting them. While listening to a very eloquent temperance lecturer, for example, Mrs. Partington, who is carried away by his oratory rather than his argument, remarks to her companion: "Dear me, how fluidly he does talk! . . . I am always rejoiced when he mounts the nostril, for his eloquence warms me in every nerve and cartridge of my body—verdigrease itself couldn't be more smooth than his blessed tongue is. . . ."[38]

Spiritualism, one of the cults then enjoying great popularity, amused Shillaber; and he good-naturedly satirized it: " 'I can't believe in spirituous knockings' said Mrs. Partington, solemnly, as some things were related to her which had been seen that appeared very mysterious. 'I can't believe about it; for I know, if Paul would come back, he would revulge himself to me here, and wouldn't make me run a mile only to get a few dry knocks. Strange that the world should be so superstitional as to believe sich a rapsody, or think a sperrit can go knocking about like a boy in vexation. *I* can't believe it, and I don't know's I could if that teapot there was to jump off the table right afore my eyes! ' "[39]

Although Shillaber was not a narrowly religious person, he did believe strongly in the practice of Christian ethics; and he frequently attacked, through Mrs. Partington, hypocrites who failed to practice what they preached. For example, when Deacon Snarl alludes pompously and piously to "the place where prayer is 'wonted' to be," Mrs. Partington says to herself: "I don't know a place under the canister of heaven where prayer is wanted to be made more than here, and I hope you'll be forgiven for the rancorous butter you sold me yesterday."[40] Another of Shillaber's favorite targets was the shallowness and hypocrisy of Victorian morality. In one of the sketches Mrs. Partington and Miss Prim, who are riding on the Chelsea Ferry, see several naked boys swimming; and, when Miss Prim expresses her vehement disapproval of their nakedness, Mrs. Partington retorts: "If the boys have no idea of impropriety I don't see why we should have. . . . This is a queer world, where we swallow mountains of impropriety in private, and choke at a bare little boy."[41]

Although Shillaber did not make a practice of using Mrs. Partington to comment satirically on political issues, he did make some exceptions, but only on issues about which he had very strong feelings. When, for example, the Know-Nothings, a secret political organization hostile to the political influence of recent immigrants and Roman Catholics, were making heavy gains in 1854 at the expense of the Democrats, Shillaber, who had no sympathy for their bigotry, used Ike and Mrs. Partington to attack them. When Ike informs his aunt that he is a Know-Nothing, she replies, "Well, you poor child, you may not know as much as some, but you ain't an idiom nuther, and though it's always well to be humble and not pretend to know things when you don't, it isn't well to go round bragging about not knowing nothing, and proving yourself a fool when folks don't suspect it. You will find full enough to do it without you." [42]

He also commented satirically through Mrs. Partington several times on the issue of slavery; and, from his comments, we know that, despite his political support of the doctrine of popular sovereignty, he personally had no sympathy for the institution of slavery. Mrs. Partington expresses his attitude toward slavery when she says, "Treat their slaves like their own children, indeed! " said Mrs. Partington as she heard the above remark made: "Well, there's no reason why they shouldn't, if all stories are true; for my part I go for abolishing all of them." [43] Unlike Artemus Ward, Shillaber was not a racist; he was convinced that the Negro, slave or free, deserved much better treatment than he received in either the North or the South. He also believed that, until the North set its own house in order and gave Negroes equal rights, Northerners had no moral right to castigate the South for its treatment of Negroes:

"What a to-do they make about treating the slaves bad at the south! " said Mrs. Partington; and everybody strained their ears to catch an opinion that perhaps was fraught with the destiny of millions. There was a slight tremor in her voice, a sort of rumbling before the "bustin" of the volcano, and her eye looked troubled as a lake by a fitful gust. "What a to-do they do make about it, to be sure! But some of our folks don't do much better. I knew a poor old colored man here in Boston that they treat jest like a nigger. People a'nt no better than scribes, pharisees, and hippogriffs, that say one thing and do another."
There is truth in thy remarks, O, most estimable Mrs. P.! Our philanthropy, we fear, if weighed in the just balance, would be found sadly wanting. [44]

When South Carolina voted at the Charleston Convention on December 20, 1860, to secede from the Union, Shillaber, who was dedicated to the Jacksonian ideal that, above all things, the federal union must be preserved, sadly commented on the act through Mrs. Partington:

"The Union must be preserved? " said Mrs. Partington, as Dr.

Spooner recited to her the toast of Gen. Jackson; "Well, it has been preserved, and now the South Catalinas are for jarring the pot over which it is preserved in, heaven bless us! There's no love of country in 'em," continued she mournfully, "and there isn't enough of the Spirit of Seventy-Six left to fill a fluid lamp." Could the Southern ear of our Confederacy have been opened at that moment to catch the rebuke that fell from those oracular lips, it would have reached the rebellious Southern heart and driven the black and ungenial blood therefrom, warming it and vivifying it into peace and fealty. Ike sat upon the floor, tearing South Carolina out of the map of the United States in his new geography, for which he was sternly reproved.[45]

Although Shillaber served as one of the editors of the Boston *Saturday Evening Gazette* until after the end of the Civil War, he did not use Mrs. Partington to express his feelings in regard to the conflict, just as he seldom employed her as a weapon in his political battles. He refrained from prostituting his character to promote causes because of his integrity as an artist and his consequent respect for Mrs. Partington as a literary creation. Until her death in 1890, as recorded in *Mrs. Partington's New Grip Sack,* Shillaber maintained his regard for her and never exploited her for commercial or political purposes.[46]

Mrs. Partington's popularity with readers was immense. Newspapers all over the United States reprinted her sayings from the Boston *Post,* and thus they reached a large and enthusiastic audience. Her success encouraged other writers to produce imitations of her monologues, and Shillaber was kept busy denying his authorship of these counterfeit pieces. Mrs. Partington appeared, for example, in 1851 as a character in *The Drummer, or New York Clerks and Country Merchants,* an anonymous play which carried on the title page the notation "Edited by Mrs. Partington."[47] In 1854, shortly before Shillaber published his first collection of Mrs. Partington's humor, Samuel P. Avery capitalized on her name by publishing a jest book entitled *Mrs. Partington's Carpet-Bag of Fun,* which included several of Shillaber's pieces that had appeared earlier in the *Post.*[48] Shillaber's own books featuring the humor of Mrs. Partington sold extremely well, and Shillaber achieved a national reputation. Until the end of his life, he received letters and requests for Mrs. Partington's autograph from those who enjoyed her humor.

The approbation which Mrs. Partington received from readers was well deserved. Her outstanding merit as a comic character lies in her style and in the firmness and the consistency with which she is drawn.

She never acts or speaks out of character. Her language, her attitudes, her habits, her mental processes, and her concerns remain constant throughout the many sketches in which she appeared over a period of forty-three years. She is also of historical significance as an authentic and convincing regional character and as a literary ancestor of the New England woman presented later in the local-color stories of Mary Wilkins Freeman and Sara Orne Jewett. Unlike most humorous characters of the nineteenth century, Mrs. Partington is remembered today not so much for her shrewd and memorable comments on contemporary public affairs as for her low-keyed whimsical humor, her homely philosophy, and, above all, for her humanity.

CHAPTER 3

Old Roger, Dr. Spooner, Blifkins, and Wideswarth

SHILLABER had to produce a considerable volume of humor to satisfy the demands of the various publications for which he wrote; and, because he was determined not to exploit Mrs. Partington for commercial ends, he limited the number of Mrs. Partington pieces he published and invented several other characters to supplement her humor. Mrs. Partington is without doubt the nonpareil of his comic characters, but Old Roger, Dr. Spooner, Blifkins, and Wideswarth—the most important of the other characters—deserve much more attention than they have received from critics and scholars. The four minor characters sometimes play subordinate roles in the anecdotes constructed around Mrs. Partington, but more often they appear singly or in various combinations in separate pieces in the pages of the *Post,* the *Carpet Bag,* and the *Saturday Evening Gazette.* Since several of Shillaber's books are primarily collections of humorous pieces which he published in periodicals, the four characters also find their way into these volumes.

Because these characters and their humor belong to the genteel tradition rather than to the vernacular, they are radically different from Mrs. Partington and her humor. The fact that they are very unlike Mrs. Partington does not mean, however, that they are decidedly inferior to her as literary creations. Indeed, a close study of the four characters provides convincing evidence that Shillaber was more imaginative and more versatile as a writer than has heretofore been assumed by critics.

I Old Roger

Old Roger, who is the central figure in scores of short humorous anecdotes scattered throughout Shillaber's work, is neither so firmly nor so clearly characterized as Mrs. Partington. A middle-aged bachelor who lives in a boardinghouse, he appears to belong to the upper middle class. His language, which is much more conventional than Mrs. Partington's, cannot be considered regional. The anecdotes in which he appears are either monologues or dialogues with his friends Philanthropos and the Brahmin Poo-Poo, with his landlady, with his fellow boarders, or with other characters. In the anecdotes, he assumes various roles. Although he is most often simply a wag or jokester, he also plays the parts of a moralist, a social critic, and a political commentator. These roles do not necessarily conflict, but neither are they entirely compatible; as a result, the reader's impression of him is blurred and uncertain.

As a wag, Old Roger inflicts puns, jokes, and conundrums on his friends, his landlady, and on the other boarders around the table. Often he joshes his landlady about the quality of food which he and the other boarders are served:

"Couldn't you get *young* pork, ma'am, to bake with your beans?" said Old Roger, somewhat cynically; as he sat at table one Sunday.

"They told me it was young! " said the landlady.

"Well, it may be so, but gray hair is not a juvenile feature, by any means, in our latitude, ma'am," continued he, fishing up a gray hair, about a foot and a half long, with his fork. "He *may* have been young, but he must have lived a very wicked life to be gray so soon."

As he spoke he looked along the table, and a slight emotion was visible among the boarders; and the man who sat opposite, with his mouth full of the edibles with which he had been endeavoring to smother a laugh, grew dark with the effort, and then collapsed, scattering dismay and crumbs amid the nicely-plaited folds of Old Roger's shirt-frills.[1]

At other times he poses conundrums for his fellow boarders to solve:

Old Roger attempted the following upon the boarders one morning. They were all sitting quietly at breakfast, when, with a most provoking smile around the corners of his mouth, as if he himself fully appreciated what he was going to say, he asked if any of them could tell him why a man deeply impressed with reverence was like a very hungry one. The idea of hunger associated with the bountiful board at which they were seated, caused the blood to rush through every vein of the landlady's body, to her face, for she felt hurt. The boarders all said they didn't know,—they couldn't see the least resemblance.

"Why," said he, chuckling, "it is because he inwardly feels a gnaw."

They couldn't understand what he meant by "an awe," and he said it was no use talking to men whose stomachs were full of the bounties of life. This he said to propitiate the landlady, who was all smiles again, as bright and sparkling as the coffee in his cup, which, catching the rays of the sun, danced, and shimmered on the wall overhead.[2]

Again, he forces atrocious puns on his captive audience around the table:

The steak was terrible one morning and Old Roger worked away at it in silence. At length his patience and masticators gave out; turning to the landlady, "Madam," said he, "your boarders should all have been umpires at horse-races."

"Why so," said she, coloring highly.

"Because, being accustomed to *'tender stakes,'* they would have none of the difficulty I experience; they could obviate it."

It was an unpardonable thing in him, thus to expose her before all the boarders, and she thought the outrage more than offset the tough meat.[3]

In Old Roger's more dignified role as social critic his most frequent target is religious hypocrisy and the perversion of the true mission of the church by people of wealth and influence. He is critical, for instance, in the following monologue of the clergyman who preaches what people want to hear rather than what they need to hear: " 'You never should blame the man who preaches in that church for crooked doctrine,' said Old Roger, after looking at one of our new and fashionable churches; 'you shouldn't blame him, for how he can preach straight, I can't see. His sermons will be as one-sided as a litter of pigs. I knew one once born in a sty with an L to it—one side was fat and t'other lean, and they were about as unhandsome and irregular a set of monsters as you ever did see, and I believe they had to kill one half of a hog at a time.' This last would seem somewhat questionable." [4]

In his role as moralist, he frequently questions popular contemporary concepts of morality in the light of true Christian precepts. In the following, he expresses his opinion of the adulatory attitude taken by many nineteenth-century people toward the wealthy philanthropist:

"To talk of a man worth his millions giving a few thousands of dollars in charity, is well enough," said Old Roger; "he should be praised for it; but what is his act compared with that of the poor woman who buys a pint of oil from her own hard earnings, and carries it in a broken-necked bottle to a sick neighbor, poorer than herself, to cheer the gloomy hours of the night? What is his act compared with hers, I should like to know? Not *that!*"

And he snapped his fingers, and felt sustained in his high estimate of the poor woman's small donation.[5]

In his role as political commentator, he generally expresses Shillaber's attitude toward current political issues. The following piece, for example, is an expression of Shillaber's belief in the unconstitutionality of the Wilmot Proviso, a resolution proposed in the House of Representatives in August, 1846, by David Wilmot which would prohibit slavery in new territories:

"Mr. Roger, this Wilmot Proviso business will fix 'em, sir, depend upon it," said the agitator decisively; "they can't spread their infernal institutions now, and slavery's black flat foot shall never pollute the free soil of the new territory; nor shall the shrieks of tortured negroes, whipped to death by cannibal slave drivers, ever be heard there; nor the clanking of the poor creatures' manacles as they go about their labor; nor—" "But," interrupted the old man, warmly "do they *want* to plant slavery there? do they want to emigrate and take their slaves there? " "To be sure they do," replied the agitator, "or why do they *oppose* the proviso so much? " "Neighbor," said Old Roger, "do you know old Squire Moon at the north end? Well, he don't go to Roxbury ever; he don't want to go; his rheumatism won't let him go; but suppose our legislature should say that he *shouldn't* go, do you think the old gentleman will be likely to be very well pleased with them? He has a right to go, which they would deprive him of, and he will insist on his right, even though he never uses it; wouldn't you do so, sir? " "Perhaps I should—but—but, good morning sir; " and they parted.[6]

II   *Dr. Spooner*

Shillaber's portrait of Dr. Spooner, as it emerges from the pages of the Boston *Saturday Evening Gazette,* is both incomplete and enigmatic. Clearly a representative of the dominant culture, he is, like Old Roger, a bachelor who lives in a boardinghouse; and, like Old Roger, too, he plays more than a single role. At various times, he is cast as a jokester, a poet, and a sage in the genteel tradition; but his roles are not completely in harmony with one another. The mindless quality of the humor which he dispenses as a wag or would-be wit, for example, is not consistent with the intellectual qualities which he displays in his role as sage. The following pun is typical of his humor: "Good books," said Dr. Spooner, "are catholic." An explanation being asked, he said, "I say so and can prove it, I think from the fact that all good books are very apt to keep Lent." [7] In his role as poet, he is the fictitious author of a series of undistinguished humorous and satirical sonnets entitled "Observations, Reflections, and Resolutions," which appeared in the pages of the *Gazette.* Typical of these sonnets is the following:

> Young friend, awake! be something if you can,
>   Lean not on others, like a sickly thing;
> Show to the world the promise of a man,
>   And take a stand now in your early spring.
> A battle is before you, and alone,
>   In conflict, single-handed you must fight,
> To wear the guerdon by the faithful won,
>   Who take a stand decisive for the right.
> 'Tis character that crowns the victor's brow,
>   And sheds its glory o'er the fleeting years;
> Then take a stand to win its circlet now,
>   While youth's bright light your opening
>   pathway cheers.
> Be something—take a stand where 'er you're
>   thrown—
> A peanut stand were better e'en than none. [8]

As a sage, Dr. Spooner plays a role which is much more serious, sophisticated, and intellectual in nature than the other two. In a series of pieces written in 1858 and 1859 Shillaber seems to have been experimenting with Dr. Spooner in an effort to create a unique character in the tradition of the nineteenth-century sage. It is quite possible that he was influenced in this effort by Oliver Wendell Holmes's *Autocrat of the Breakfast Table,* which had appeared serially in the *Atlantic Monthly* in 1857—58 and which had been published as a book in 1858. Whether or not the Autocrat exerted any influence on Shillaber, Dr. Spooner displays several of the basic characteristics of Holmes's fictional character. Like the Autocrat, Dr. Spooner enjoys discoursing on any topic, and he often displays his wisdom at a boardinghouse table. Philosophically, however, he is much closer to Emerson's idealism than to Holmes's rationalism. Like Emerson, for example, Dr. Spooner is firmly convinced that genius is not the result of cultivating the rational mind; for, in one of his monologues, he says: "Take care of the intellect; educate it to the extent of your ability; but genius is a spring of water that will gush up spontaneously through the cultivation, and add grace thereto." [9] In another piece entitled "The Intellect," he develops the idea that great men are not necessarily the most highly intellectual men. Like Emerson in "The American Scholar," Dr. Spooner speaks against withdrawal from the world and expresses the belief that experience is much more important than books in attaining wisdom:

"The cultivation of the intellect," said Dr. Spooner, bringing his left hand upon the back of his right as he stood leaning on his cane, "is excellent, but we should not forget as many are too apt, that the intellect is but one of the many things that go to make up the perfect man. The wisest men of the world have not been intellectual men, necessarily. Experience teaches more than books, and though men cram themselves intellectually and can repeat every word that has been written, except that they have counterbalancing qualities, they are no more worthy of praise than a New Zealander, who to gratify his epicurean palate stuffs himself to repletion on whales, of the Tom Hyers and Heenans who pet their knuckles and muscles as the great principles that make the man...." [10]

A few months later in a piece entitled "Too High," Dr. Spooner again stressed the dangers inherent in developing the intellect at the expense of other faculties:

"I think," said Dr. Spooner, taking a pinch of snuff out of Mrs. Partington's box, "that men may in intellectual progression get too high, and prove, in the lofty atmosphere in which they sail, tied to earth by a single thread of interest, nothing but intellectual kites, looking grandly up there in the brighter sunshine, but isolated and alone. They get so accustomed to living in that higher atmosphere, that they grow restive when drawn nearer earth, as a kite seems to struggle with an effort to free itself when approaching the hand.... Knowledge is a realm of words and facts—cold and pragmatical; wisdom is a garden of utilities, and loves, and tastes, and sympathies. To choose between them I would have Wisdom." [11]

Some of Dr. Spooner's other ideas also have a distinctly Emersonian ring to them. In a discourse entitled "Individuality," for example, he expresses his belief that, although each human being is a microcosm of the universe, he is also an individual with qualities unique to him:

"I love to stand at the street corners," said Dr. Spooner, as he was standing, with his cane behind him, on which he was leaning, looking up and down the street. "Did the fact never occur to you," continued he, "that every one of those persons moving before you was an individuality, an atomic component in the great aggregated humanity, and yet an isolation, a microcosmatic existence in a world of existences? " He looked at us a moment, as if expecting an answer. Overwhelmed by the profundity of the question, we remained silent. "Yes," continued he, lifting himself up by his cane, "each individual is an individual world. All the love, hope, ambition, hatred, and devotion, revealed in the grand macrocosm before us—the world—is enacted in each little globe that moves by us,—forming the microcosm—the individual. It is a grand study, sir. Man, abstractly considered, is a broad sweep of the human horizon with the glass of truth; individually considered, the telescope is reversed,—revealing man infinitely less, but still the same. I have stood here, by the hour, reading the faces that have moved by me as the planets move round the sun, presenting varied phases,—one little world presenting the mirthful phase, another the sad, another the anxious, another the fierce,—but how distinct and beautiful the individuality! At such times I think of the music of the lines describing the 'solemn silence' with which the planets revolve,
'Forever singing, as they shine,
The hand that made us is divine.'
These sing to me in their distinctness and silence, and"—A boy passing at the time touched the Doctor's cane, and, it being just when he was drawing himself up to give emphasis to his sentence, he fell backward, with considerable violence. He smiled as he gathered himself up. "Human weakness," said he, "may fall, but eternal truth must stand." [1] [2]

He takes issue in "Who Is Vile? " with a female boarder who condemns another woman as "a vile creature." The Doctor, who asks her to be charitable, argues that good is an inward, spiritual quality not to be measured by outward appearances and that the seed of perfection lies in all of us:

"She's a vile creature," said the severe woman, looking very red in the face. The conversation had been upon the propriety of recognizing one who had fallen from virtue, if fame were to be believed, and the severe woman, whose purity could not be questioned, closed her side of the argument with the remark commencing this paragraph. Dr. Spooner arose from the table and stepped behind his chair, as children do in schools when called upon to recite. "The term vile, madam," said he, looking at the severe woman, "is a very strong one coming from human lips, and those who utter it should be very sure that they stand on sure ground themselves. Because great imperfection may be imputed to any one, it does not follow that the whole body is corrupt. There may be beneath all this corruption a stratum of pure soil, in which good seeds may grow,—in which, indeed, they may be now germinating,—that may not shoot their leaf up through the crust of sin and degradation that keeps them down, but may throw out the tendrils of an undying principle, that, deeper than the flesh, will one day find an outgrowth in other airs, and shame those who, wrapt in their own sensuous perfectibility, have not allowed a spiritual seed to grow. Vile, indeed! The expression comes with a poor grace from any unless they have the scale and balance by a special patent from heaven with which to weigh human wrong, and it should be carefully used. I once knew a case where a good woman and a bad woman made custards for a sick person, and both met in the sick room—the one with a proud spirit that she was not like the wicked one, the other humble and retiring, as if ashamed of herself. But the good woman's custards were made of skimmed milk and sweetened with brown sugar, and the bad woman's were made very deliciously; and the sick one fancied that the souls of both those persons were seen in the custard-cups; and in the comparative estimate he found more intrinsic excellence in the bad woman than in the good woman, and believed, as he still believes, that many transgressions, that spring from human weakness, will be forgiven, for the sparks of love that may be still smouldering deeply within. I see you laugh at my homely illustration; but it is a life-picture, treat it as you may. Let us call them unfortunate, rather than vile, and humble ourselves to regard them with charity."

The severe woman looked very red, but said nothing further till the doctor was gone.[13]

Dr. Spooner is also the hero of a poem of sixty-eight stanzas entitled "The Modern Syntax; Dr. Spooner in search of the Delectable." The poem, which is a takeoff on William Combe's satirical poem "Dr. Syntax in Search of the Picturesque," was published serially in the *Gazette* and later collected in *Partingtonian Patchwork*. In the poem Dr. Spooner searches frantically for happiness in books, politics, social life, trade, education, religion, and in various other areas of human activity. After a long and arduous search, he finally discovers that the happiness he is looking for lies only within himself:

LXV

And then despairingly he made complaint:
  "Oh! who can tell me where is happiness?
With much endeavor I am worn and faint,
  And each step seems to show the progress less
In striving for that boon which hope did paint,
  Which seems more distant as my steps I press.
Tell me, ye wise ones, in earth's mighty bound,
Where, tell me where, may happiness be found? "

LXVI

"Here stay your steps, my boy," a veteran spoke;
  "I'm just the chap 'll point you to the spot;
I've sought for happiness through fire and smoke—
  My brierwood pipe—and here is where I've got:
The search for happiness is but a joke,
  For which you needn't go all round the lot;
I'll ease your caput of its great quandary—
For delectation—see the dictionary." [14]

Since Shillaber never uses Dr. Spooner as an alter ego and since the tone of the Spooner pieces is uncertain and inconsistent, it is difficult to decide how seriously the reader should accept the ideas of his character. Although Shillaber at times seems to be in sympathy with the ideas expressed by Dr. Spooner, at other times he seems to be poking fun at him. Shillaber's ambivalent attitude toward Dr. Spooner is evident in an anecdote entitled "Industry" in which Dr. Spooner earnestly lectures Mr. Plane, a carpenter who is working for him, on the fallaciousness of the American notion that all industry is virtuous; but when the carpenter agrees with him and lays down his tools, the Doctor looks rather foolish:

"I love to see people industrious," remarked Mr. Plane, the carpenter, giving a finishing knock at a clapboard nail he was driving, as though he were putting it as a period to his sentence. "So do I," said Dr. Spooner, "but perhaps we would not agree with regard to our definition of the word industry. I do not believe that industry is slavish devotion to work, that never allows a moment's respite from toil, that from early morning to night devotes itself, might and main, hammer and tongs, speaking after the manner of men, to one pursuit—that is not my idea of industry. . . . There is an old saying that it is better to wear out than rust out, but, between you and I, I think I shall allow myself to rust a little." "I think I shall," said the carpenter, laying down his hammer. "I like your theory, sir, and as you are so kind, I shall leave clapboarding your barn for this afternoon and go fishing." "Ah," replied the Doctor, "that alters the case materially, and if the work is not done by tomorrow night, you will receive no dimes therefor. In this particular case a little industry is a great virtue." The Doctor turned away, and the carpenter, with an expressive wink at his journeyman, resumed his hammer and the work was done.[15]

Altogether, then, Shillaber's portrait of Dr. Spooner is ambiguous and incomplete. Whatever he may have had in mind in creating Dr. Spooner, he ceased experimenting with him and turned to more purely journalistic endeavors when the secession movement began and the nation drifted toward the Civil War.

III *Blifkins*

As a literary creation, Benjamin Blifkins is much superior to Old Roger and Dr. Spooner; and, with the exception of Mrs. Partington and Ike, he is the most successful comic character in Shillaber's humor. Much more modern in concept than Mrs. Partington, he has more in common with James Thurber's or Robert Benchley's worried Little Man than he does with the homespun oracles of the nineteenth century. A member of the urban middle class, he owns an interest in a store, he is continually harassed by his wife, he is frustrated by his own inadequacies, and he is defeated by inanimate objects. His wife, who is unduly concerned with status, is cruel and relentless in intensifying his feeling of incompetency. Unlike Thurber and Benchley, Shillaber, of course, knew nothing of the psychological theories of Freud and Jung; but he nonetheless had a penetrating insight into the tensions and frustrations inherent in marriage, and he used this knowledge to good advantage in his tales concerning the troubles and trials of Benjamin Blifkins.

Shillaber published a series of stories about Blifkins in the *Gazette*, the best of which he later collected in *Partingtonian Patchwork* under the heading "The Blifkins Papers." In these "papers," which can best be classified as tales, Shillaber either presents the action from Blifkins's point of view or employs a "frame" technique in which Blifkins's story is framed by an introduction and a conclusion which are presented through the voice of the author-narrator. The plots, which are uncomplicated, are usually constructed around two conflicts: Blifkins's unsuccessful attempts to come to grips with some trivial but irritating dilemma which confronts him, and his wife's constant efforts to destroy his self-confidence. The following tale, entitled "Blifkins the Mechanic," is typical of the Blifkins series:

"Mr. Blifkins," said my wife, on the morning of washing day, "Bridget complains that something is the matter with the soft-water pump."

"Well, my dear," I replied,—I am very careful to put in all the little tender terms on washing days, having found them serve admirably as mollifiers at such times,—"I will see about it."

I had not quite finished reading my morning paper, and sat a moment to conclude the account of the last fearful casualty, when Bridget's face was thrust into the door, as red and bright as an old-fashioned brass warming-pan.

"Indade, mem," said she, "the pump's gone again."

"I wish you was," arose to my lips, but I didn't speak it.

"Well," replied my wife, "I've done all I could about it, unless I am expected to draw the box and fix it. I expect every day when I shall have to do such work. A woman's life is hard enough at the best, but a little additional service would not hurt her, I dare say. Perhaps, in the intervals of household duties, she might take in jobs of pump-mending."

I said nothing.

"Mr. Blifkins," said my wife, "will you see to the pump? "

This was said in a tone that completely overcame the horror awakened by the casualty, and throwing the paper aside, I proceeded to the kitchen. I tried the handle of the pump, and, sure enough, the water refused to flow. A few drops only oozed from the nose, and, as I plied the handle, the pump gave forth a rumbling sound, as though it were surly in its refusal to yield the accustomed supply.

"This is a pretty state of things for washing day! " said my wife.

"Well, my dear," said I, "I don't see how you can blame me for it. 'Thou canst not say I did it.' "

I immediately essayed to take out the box. The screws that secured the top were rusty, and refused to turn.

"Mrs. Blifkins," said I, "where is the hammer? "

"How should I know where the hammer is? " she replied, "It is probably where you used it last. You leave every thing for me to take care of. My father used to say, 'A place for every thing and every thing in its place.' I wish *all* men were as particular.''

I remembered that I had used the hammer to repair a chicken-coop some weeks before, and, proceeding to the spot, I found it, rusty and dirty, lying just where I had left it. A system like this, closely followed, would prove of immense advantage; for a memory of where an article was used would immediately suggest the spot where it was to be found. Returning to the kitchen, I commenced work. The rusty threads of the screws refused persistently to yield; but patience wins; and after a half hour's sweating and fretting, I had the top removed, and the pump-box in my hand. There were evident signs of decay in the leather; and bringing my natural ingenuity to bear upon it, I hammered, and tacked, and cut, and pulled, until I fancied that I had attained perfection in my effort.

"Mrs. Blifkins," says I, in my momentary satisfaction, "can you tell me the difference betwixt a man who mends pumps and a prune? "

Of course she couldn't; and I told her that one was a plum and the other was a plumber; whereat she was pleased to smile, though, I thought, rather derisively.

"Now we shall see," says I, putting in the box, "the triumph of genius. Pour in some water, Bridget, and as I pump, you shall see the water flow."

I manned the brakes; but in vain my effort. No effect was produced but the most painful sound—a sort of asthmatic wheezing, like that of a porcine quadruped just expiring under the effect of a surgical operation upon his neck. My triumph changed, and my chipper notes partook of a more tempestuous character, as I muttered an expression that nothing but the immediate circumstances could justify.

"That's right," said my wife; "I would talk in that way. It will help the matter, I dare say, very much. Men have got no patience. If they had to bear as much as women do, I don't know what would become of them."

"I will bring mechanics," said I, a little subdued, "and they shall bring the pump."

I immediately sought Lumb.

"Send workmen," said I, "O man of lead pipe and solder, and mend that without which washing day becomes a Sabbath without a sermon—for what were washing day without water? "

Two men accompanied me to my home—philanthropists, with disposition and ability to relieve the difficulty under which I labored.

"Now, my boys," said I, as I introduced them to the field of their operations, "put her through."

The term "her" struck Mrs. Blifkins as irrelevant, and somewhat personal, as I judged from her looks. No barometer could be more exact than was her countenance to my experienced vision.

"Look here, sir," said one of the men, trying the handle; "there ain't nothing the matter with the pump."

"Then what is the bother with the infernal thing? " I asked, excitedly.

"The principal reason is, I think, sir, that the cistern has gin out."

I looked at the man wonderingly; but his honest eye convinced me that he was sincere, and after examination proved the truth of what he said.

"My friend," said I, "here is a trifle for you, and I will settle with Lumb. Don't say any thing about it."

I never knew how the matter came out, but always thought Mrs. Blifkins must have told of it.[16]

The humor in the tales arises both from the predicaments in which Blifkins finds himself and from his generally futile attempts to cope with them. The victim of a domineering wife and of his own lack of courage, Blifkins is constantly badgered by Mrs. Blifkins, who both takes advantage of his timidity to get her own way and enjoys taunting him about his own inadequacies. Subsequent events may prove that Blifkins was originally right, but his wife resolutely refuses to admit it. In "Blifkins' Summer Retreat," for example, Mrs. Blifkins, in spite of her husband's objections, is determined to spend a vacation in the country because she wants to keep up with the Joneses. Since they cannot afford to go to Saratoga or to the White Mountains, she arranges for the family to spend a fortnight in the home of a miserly Yankee farmer. Blifkins is miserable. They are fed skim milk and fat pork, they must retire at sundown, and Blifkins cannot sleep because of the noise made by the farm animals. Although Mrs. Blifkins is no doubt as unhappy and uncomfortable as her husband, she, for the sake of victory, is willing to endure it without complaint.[17]

As a householder Blifkins is exceedingly inept, and Mrs. Blifkins compounds his frustrations by reminding him constantly of his inability to solve the multitudinous domestic problems which beset him. In "Blifkins the Householder," he faces the task of removing the snow from his sidewalk; and for some reason the snow always falls more heavily on his property than on that of his neighbors. Mrs. Blifkins insists, of course, that he must remove the snow himself, and, as he works, she continually torments him. Much to her satisfaction, the project ends in complete disaster:

"Mr. Blifkins," said my wife, "why don't you go out, now, and shovel it off yourself? " Said I, in reply, "Your counsel is excellent, and I think I will." I at once proceeded to prepare myself for the task; but before I could get ready, there were five applications for the job and five refusals. I pulled on a pair of long boots, tied a comforter round my ears, and went out. "You're going to pitch into it, I see," said a voice, as I began. 'Twas one of the policemen, and he looked, I thought, rather disappointed. "You don't catch me this time," said I. I commenced vigorously, throwing the snow aside with "heart of controversy." But I began too fast. The fifth shovelful assured me that I had reckoned without my host; and I was almost tempted to abandon my undertaking by the offer of a deluding Hibernian gentleman, who insinuated that he might shovel it "off for a quarter of a dollar." But an incidental remark seemed to reflect on my ability to perform the task, and I bade him depart. "Are you almost done? " said my wife from the upper window. How unreasonable these women are! I pitched in, not deigning a reply. I grew very hot, realizing the philosophical fact of there being heat in snow; strange I never noticed it before! "Don't shovel the snow against the house! " said my wife from the upper window. At that instant an avalanche came from the roof, burying me in the snowy grave I had just been digging. "Did it hurt you much? " asked my wife from her upper point of observation. I replied to her, as soon as I could free myself, that it did not, and playfully essayed to throw a shoveful of snow at her. It fell short of its mark; but the shovel found its way through three squares of my parlor window. "Save the pieces! " said my wife in an ironical tone. I looked at my damaged property with bitterness of spirit. It occurred to me that my neighbor's snow-shovel was better than mine, and I went to borrow it. When I returned, I found that someone had stolen my own shovel in my absence. In a rage I smote the pave with the borrowed one, and broke it off short in the handle, with a remark that sounded something like profanity. At this I withdrew from the field, determined to employ the first one who came along who wished to shovel me out. I waited all the forenoon, but no one came. It was wonderful how they managed to keep away. In the afternoon I received a summons to appear before the police court by the hands of one of my watchful policemen, and have just returned from that august tribunal, where I have paid three dollars, without costs. So, reckoning my labor, the lost time, the stolen shovel, the broken one, the smashed window, the three dollars, and the aggravation, I think it don't pay.[18]

In "Blifkins and the Cat," he is awakened early on a Sunday morning by his wife who with some satisfaction tells him that there is a dead cat in front of the house which he must dispose of. Poor Blifkins is at a complete loss to know what to do with it. Should he throw it in the street, or should he bury it in the yard? As usual, Mrs. Blifkins taunts him about his inability to deal with the situation. He finally solves the problem by paying a boy to carry the cat away, only to be humiliated when he discovers that the boy had thrown the cat in the yard in the first place in the belief that Blifkins would pay him to dispose of it.[19]

Against the wishes of his wife Blifkins decides in "Blifkins the Horticulturist" to improve the appearance of his grounds by planting a grapevine. After purchasing a scion about the size of a lead pencil, he confidently takes it home to plant it. An Irishman, however, persuades Blifkins to hire him to plant it. The Irishman digs a huge hole, persuades him to buy two loads of fertilizer, and overcharges him for his labor. Blifkins has suffered another defeat.[20]

Sometimes, however, like Thurber's Little Man, Blifkins becomes aggressive, rebels against his wife's domination, and defeats her, at least for the moment. In "Blifkins Takes A Stand," for example, he yields when his wife objects to his smoking in the house; and he endures her derision when he fails in his attempt to make some household repairs; but, when she attempts to tell him how to shave, he stands his ground:

"Mrs. Blifkins," I cried with some heat, as the razor scored a half-inch incision into my cuticle, "anything but this. You may be boss in every department of the household, from the mending of coal-pens and sawing of wood to the blacking of boots and hanging of clothes-lines; but here is a job that I choose to boss myself. I feel that it is an operation quite outside of your sphere. Nature, Mrs. Blifkins, has fixed bounds here—settled them to a hair—by depriving you of the beard that is such a delightful ornament to the masculine sex; and it is full bad enough to have to take care of it without female inter-ference."[21]

But Blifkins's misfortunes and inadequacies extend beyond the realm of marriage and his household. Although Shillaber's characterization of Blifkins is not, like Thurber's portrait of his Little Man, based on a deterministic philosophy, Blifkins does seem to encounter more ill fortune than he deserves. Try as he may, he seems unable to avoid involvement in situations which embarrass and frustrate him. In "Blifkins the Mourner," for instance, he dutifully sets out to attend the funeral of a friend named Whiffletree. After losing his way, he finally locates a funeral, sits reverently through the service, comforts the relatives of the deceased, and rides to the cemetery with the mourners only to discover at the graveside that he has attended the wrong funeral:

Gathering in a solemn circle, amid the most impressive stillness, each stepped forward to take the last look. It was Blifkins's turn, and with demure countenance, he prepared to take his final leave of his friend, when, as he looked into the stony face before him, he saw, not Whiffletree, but Deacon Hardhead, a man whose reputation for closeness had won him a name by no means desirable, and who once had become possessed of a note of Blifkins's which he pressed with most persistent energy till he paid it, putting him to some considerable inconvenience to raise the funds at a time when money was scarce. Blifkins had hated him cordially ever since; and to find himself now one of a retinue to do him honor, and his friend Whiffletree denied his tribute, caused him a feeling that he could not overcome. Even his fair companion could not reconcile him to the false position he was in,—at the *wrong funeral*,—and stopping the carriage at the first railway track, he rode to town in the horse-car, feeling that he had been outrageously swindled.[22]

In "Mr. Blifkins sees Kean," he decides that he must take Mrs. Blifkins to the theater to see a dramatic production in which Charles Kean, a popular actor, is playing. After experiencing great difficulty in securing tickets and getting to the theater, he and his wife sit through the play only to discover that they are at the wrong theater and that the actor whom they believed to be Kean is not the famous man at all:

"Ah, Blifkins, you here? " said his friend Jolliboy, coming forward and shaking him by the hand; "and Mrs. Blifkins! I declare this is an unexpected pleasure."

"Yes," said Mrs. Blifkins; "Benjamin wished to see Kean, and I thought it would be a relief from household cares to come with him."

Blifkins didn't think this was putting it quite right, but said nothing in reply, merely remarking to Jolliboy,—

"He plays very well for an old man."

"Not so old, either," said Jolliboy, who at fifty was still laying claim to juvenility.

"Why, he must be near sixty—over fifty, at least," said Blifkins, mentally calculating the difference of time betwixt then and now.

"Why, no," replied Jolliboy; "it can't be more than twenty years since he went to school in South Boston."

"Who? " said Blifkins; "Charles Kean? "

"No, Frank Mayo," replied Jolliboy; "what has Charles Kean to do with it? "

"Oh, nothing! " said Blifkins, squeezing Mrs. Blifkins's arm in order to keep her from saying any thing, seeing that he had made a mistake; "nothing, only I was thinking of Kean at the moment—that's all."

"I never saw the character of Charles de Moor played better," said Jolliboy, enthusiastically.

"Nor I," responded Blifkins.

Mrs. Blifkins said nothing.[23]

Blifkins is an interesting comic character, partly, at least, because he is a prototype of the twentieth-century Little Man rather than a crackerbarrel oracle or a fool character in the homespun tradition. Like Benchley's Little Man, he is baffled by the problems of everyday living, harassed by his children, and continually rebuffed and embarrassed by nearly everyone with whom he comes in contact. And, like Thurber's Little Man, he is victimized by his wife, by gadgets, and by his own nature. It is true, of course, that Shillaber did not—indeed, could not—present his portrait of Blifkins within the same philosophical and psychological frames of reference which Thurber and Benchley used, but nevertheless the resemblances between Blifkins and the Little Man are unmistakable.

IV *Wideswarth*

The character of Wideswarth emerges almost entirely in a long series of sonnets which Shillaber wrote from Wideswarth's point of view and published under his name in the *Post* and *Saturday Evening Gazette*.[24] Fifty-three of the best of the Wideswarth sonnets he collected in *Rhymes With Reason and Without*. Although he appears as "Professor" Wideswarth in several of the Partington pieces, his role in these pieces is so insignificant that he is little more than a name. It is true that there are some inconsistencies in the character of Wideswarth as revealed in

the sonnets; but, despite the inconsistencies, he emerges as a fairly clear
and distinct figure. The name Wideswarth is, of course, a takeoff on
Wordsworth; and his use of the Shakespearean sonnet, a favorite form
of Wordsworth and the other Romantics, suggests that he envisions
himself as a Romantic poet. Indeed, Shillaber uses Wideswarth, who is
excessively and comically Romantic, to poke fun at those who take too
literally the Romantic concept of an ideal world.

A slave of Romantic art and his own fantasies, Wideswarth is a
dilettante whose grip on actuality is very tenuous and who consequently finds the real world an unhappy place in which to live. A
misfit, he is lonely, impractical, unrealistic, egotistical, and alienated.
Although his Romantic expectations are constantly crushed, he
perseveres in his determination to live only in the ideal; as a result, he
lives a sterile and meaningless existence: his responses to nature are
artificial; his relationships with other people are superficial; and his
image of himself is false.

Although Wideswarth is firmly convinced that he truly loves external
nature, his responses to nature, rather than being individual and
genuine, are stock ones based upon his superficial reading of Romantic
verse about nature. A sonnet entitled "The Snow" illustrates his typical
response to nature and his subsequent shock when reality intrudes upon
his sentimental reverie:

> Now white and beautiful creation lies,
>   Nursing its struggling germs beneath the veil;
> On rushing wings the fairy snow-flake flies,
>   Urged by the breath of the on-hurrying gale.
> Now jingling bells thrill wildly on the ear,
>   As vying coursers dart along the way,
> Now rise in chorus tones of blithest cheer,
>   As beams the moon with calm, untroubled ray.
> I bless the snow! How fair its glittering sheen,
>   How pure and holy is its pearly light!
> Clad in its robe, the earth looks like a queen
>   In the chaste vesture of her bridal night.
> 'Tis passing fair,—yet, hardly fair is that,—
> An avalanche, confound it, crushes in my hat! [25]

In "To Spring" Wideswarth reacts in the same sentimental fashion to
the natural beauty of the season. Following an apostrophe to spring, he
tells how he opens his window so that he can breathe the "vernal air"
and share in the "vestal favors" of spring. From the protection of the

window, he listens to the bleating of the spring lambs, sees the violets in the "verdant fields," and smells the perfume of the "myriad blossoms which the season yields." Then, however, instead of rushing outdoors in his disarray and surrendering his senses and his soul to the seductiveness of spring, he calls to his maid to bring his cloak and gloves. He will walk forth sedately to meet nature on a very formal and artificial basis:

> The shooting vine hangs trembling in the breeze
> And buds luxuriant grace the teeming bough,
> The robin sings his song amid the trees,
> And Nature pours her notes melodious now.
> O, Spring! Thy beauty admiration moves,
> But—but—but—Mary, bring my cloak and gloves! [26]

Wideswarth in "Sunset" responds to the quiet beauty of a summer evening, not through his own sensibility, but through his memory of the mood of Thomas Gray's "Elegy Written in a Country Churchyard." Altogether trite and derivative, the sonnet is a very weak and ineffective echo of Gray's "Elegy":

> The Sun is sinking in the radiant West,
> And over woods, and fields, and glassy streams,
> Are thrown the glories of his ruddy beams,
> Which earth with richer loveliness invest;
> And softening influences mark the hour, —
> The cattle meekly take their march for home,
> And low responsive to the sounds which come
> Proclaiming gentle Evening's sovereign power.
> Down 'mid the trees the golden sunshine floats,
> And the sad fife-bird pours his sweetest lay
> The robin sings his vespers on the spray,
> And myriad insects trill their pensive notes.
> The Sun sinks slowly to his watery bed,
> And draws a cap of cloud about his weary head. [27]

In "Church Music" Wideswarth is transported into the realm of the ideal by the grandeur of the church architecture and by the music of the church organ:

> Ah, dearly do I love the organ's pealing
> With psalm-tune holy or with anthem grand,
> The while I drum the measure with my hand,

> And gaze devoutly at the frescoed ceiling,
> Where modern Angelos have spent their skill,
> And mimic niche and pillar make display,
> And shadows fling themselves in every way,
> In independence of the sun's high will.

He is cruelly jolted back to reality, however, when the harsh sounds of nature and humanity intrude themselves: "Bang goes a cricket! —Squalls a child sonorous, / And earth's harsh discord drowns the heavenly chorus." [28]

Wideswarth, whose relationships with people are as false and fleeting as his kinship with nature, is able to forge a meaningful alliance with no other human being, male or female. Selfish and self-centered, he is altogether incapable of meeting the demands of either love or friendship. In a sonnet entitled "On a Picture of Lillie" he reveals his emotional immaturity by rhapsodizing over a picture of a child with which he has become infatuated. Idealizing not only the likeness of the child but childhood itself, he writes:

> A truthful page is childhood's lovely face
>   Whereon sweet Innocence has record made,—
> An outward semblance of the heart's young grace,
>   Where truth, and love, and trust, are all portrayed!
> O, blessed childhood! Like the wakening day,
>   The auroral flush bespeaks thy rising sun,
> And spreads a roseate tint about thy way,
>   And Hope's gay blossoms open one by one. [29]

He responds in "Lips" to the trite image, which he has found in a poem or painting, of a rosebud between the lips of a young woman. Rapturously, he writes:

> I saw a rose-bud 'twixt a maiden's lips—
>   Borrowing new beauties from its ruby throne,
>   And adding them to graces of its own,—
> A bud the like the wild bee oftenest sips.
> The sweetness of her lips did seem to lend
>   A better fragrance than the bud possessed,
>   And, as it on its station blest,
> 'Twas joy to see their mutual beauties blend. [30]

But reality intrudes upon his fantasy when by a link of association he recalls an unpleasant experience which he had had as a youth when, during a kissing game, he had to pay forfeit by kissing "a somewhat antiquated maid" who suffered from halitosis.

Wideswarth's extreme loneliness is apparent in "In Strange Company," a sonnet in which he tells of riding on an omnibus with a young woman on Thanksgiving Day. Although he neither knows her name nor converses with her, he imagines her to be a perfect specimen of womanhood:

> But she was chaste as ice, and pure as snow,
>   And I could vow, though I knew not her name,
>   Reproach ne'er dared to meddle with her fame,—
> I pride myself a virtuous dame to know.[31]

Pathetically unaware that he is reacting, not to a real woman, but to his own idealization of the other sex, Wideswarth convinces himself that he has had a rare and gratifying experience.

In "The Dance," Wideswarth's feelings of loneliness and alienation are intensified by the sights and sounds of a lively dance in a nearby ballroom; but he comforts himself with the thought that, when the ball is over, the revelers' lives will be as plagued by care and worry as is his own:

> The lamps in yonder hall glow grandly bright,
>   And music 'liveneth the midnight air,
>   And white-robed forms, than seraphs' scarce less fair,
> Whirl fast and graceful 'twixt me and the light.
> There youth and beauty crowd upon my sight,
>   As through my half-closed curtains forth I gaze,
>   To watch the sportive thread the giddy maze,
> And smile in sympathy with their delight.
> Delicious hour!—enchantment rules the night;
>   The outside world is herein all forgot,—
> *Here* is their world, and pleasure all its lot,
> And images of ill have taken flight.
> Took flight?—ah, no,—they only wait outside,
> To join them in the coach, as home they ride.[32]

The reasons for Wideswarth's loneliness are clearly expressed in "Friendship." After an apostrophe to friendship, he turns to the ideals of friendship in the Damon and Pythias story; and then he moves to the world of his contemporary stage, citing the noble savage Metamora in

John Augustus Stone's melodrama *Metamora or the Last of the Wampanoags*. Edwin Forrest's impersonation of the Indian who declaims his friendship for all white men seems to appeal to Wideswarth more directly than anything he can find in the life about him. He then expresses regret that noble comradeship is no longer possible because would-be friends "are men of quite a different sort of mould, / And buying oftener than 'getting sold,' / Asking more always than they wish to give." Sadly, he concludes that friendship is so demanding and exacting that "The fewer friends one has by far the better." [33]

A basic cause of Wideswarth's inability to live successfully in the real world and to establish meaningful relationships with other people is the fact that he has a false image of himself. Selfish and conceited, he greatly overrates his own ability and his own worth. In "Webster vs. Wideswarth," for example, he complains bitterly because people admire and applaud Daniel Webster, the great stateman and orator, but completely ignore Wideswarth. Poets like himself, he believes, deserve as much recognition as do statesmen like Webster:

> And I'm content, for one, to bear my part,—
> Content, too, that the meed be likewise borne
> By all who merit it, with all my heart.
> But Webster takes the whole, nor leaves for me
> One single leaf from the undying tree.[34]

His overpowering egotism will not allow him to see himself as the poetaster and dilettante that he is.

Because, like Thurber's Walter Mitty, Wideswarth is unable to meet the demands of the real world, he often retreats into the realm of fantasy where he can play roles which are denied him in real life. He imagines in "Riding," for example, that he is a rich man traveling grandly in a coach rather than a poorer man riding in a public omnibus. As he rides along, he allows his imagination free play. Fancying himself a benevolent man of wealth who wishes to make life easier for people less fortunate than himself, he imagines that he welcomes aboard his coach a crippled man, an elderly woman, and a "sweet damsel" with a "blooming face." His false image of himself is punctured, however, when he is rudely asked to pay his fare:

> My coach has room enough on every side,
> And he shall fill it, please he, day by day.
> Come in, my crippled friend, we'll find you place;

And you, stout lady, slow with fat and age,
Here you the ills of gout or corns may 'suage;
Come in, sweet damsel with the blooming face;
Come in; what's this? What, hold your hand for pay?
A "bus," i' faith! thus grandeur's dreams decay! [35]

In "Philanthropy," Wideswarth imagines that he is a game hunter. Although he fancies himself a hunter of birds rather than lions or Cape buffaloes, he enacts a role similar to that played by the hero of Ernest Hemingway's "The Short Happy Life of Francis Macomber." Training his gun on a fat bird "warbling on the waning bough," he finds that he does not have the necessary courage to pull the trigger. He attempts to overcome his cowardice by imagining that he is a hardened veteran of the recent Mexican War: "I do detest to kill thee—manhood shrinks / That late could shoot a man in Mexico, / And unrelenting cause his blood to flow." While he is screwing up his courage, however, the bird flies from the tree, and Wideswarth comforts himself with the thought that the bird must have flown because he sensed the terrible danger he was in: "I must, -but hang the bird! he's flown away, / It wasn't safe for him round here to stay." [36]

Using Wideswarth as a satirical weapon, Shillaber attacked in a comic way the sentimental poetaster who, entirely misunderstanding the Romantic concept of ideality, tried to live in an ideal realm of his own imagining rather than in the world of actuality. Subtler than the satire usually found in the columns of newspapers, that of the Wideswarth sonnets is directed at the perversion of one of the prime tenets of nineteenth-century Romanticism. Although the satire is both amusing and effective, it seems certain that the average newspaper reader of the time would understand and enjoy Shillaber's sentimental and didactic newspaper verse much more than he would appreciate the Wideswarth sonnets.

CHAPTER 4

Ike Partington and Books for Boys

SHILLABER created Ike Partington in 1848 primarily as a foil to Mrs. Partington in an effort to enliven the anecdotes which he was writing for his column in the Boston *Post*. Although in the beginning Ike was little more than a name, he gradually became as lifelike as Mrs. Partington herself, and he played a prominent role not only in the Partington anecdotes but also in a series of books for boys. But, since Shillaber created Ike as an antagonist to the typical hero of contemporary books for boys as well as foil to Mrs. Partington, it is helpful to know something of the general nature of mid-nineteenth-century juvenile fiction.

The field of children's literature in the United States in 1848 presented a dismal prospect. Although many books for boys and girls were being written, they were generally intended to reinforce the dominant culture rather than to appeal to the natural interests of children. Strongly didactic and moralistic, they were designed to inculcate in children the established values of duty, obedience, honesty, industry, thrift, temperance, generosity, piety, and patriotism. Very popular, with parents and teachers at least, the "Sunday-school" books, sponsored by the American Tract Society, reached a large audience. Poorly written and filled with sentimental platitudes, they helped for decades to put a blight on the writing of good juvenile fiction.

In addition to the Sunday-school books, numerous volumes of didactic fiction were issued by publishers for children and adolescents. Two of the most popular series for boys were the Peter Parley and the Little Rollo books. Samuel Goodrich, who wrote most of the Peter Parley books, published the first of the series in Boston in 1827.[1] The books were generally well written, but since they were designed to dispense information, teach right conduct, and encourage patriotism rather than to delight children, they made very dull and tedious reading. Since Shillaber worked for Tuttle and Weeks, the firm which printed the Peter Parley books, he was most certainly well acquainted with the series.

The Little Rollo series, inaugurated in 1832 by Jacob Abbott and published by Harpers, was also primarily didactic in intention.[2] Abbott's objectives in the series were to inform children about other countries, to convince them of the superiority of the United States, to encourage them to work and think, and to develop in them a respect for authority. Because Abbott avoided the fanciful and the imaginative, his books, too, are lacking in freedom, vigor, and interest. Like the unrealistic heroes of most contemporary books for boys and of the didactic tales which abounded in magazines, spelling books, and readers, Peter Parley and Little Rollo are sober, industrious, well-behaved, and eager to improve their minds and characters.

I *Ike Partington*

The didactic school was predicated upon the assumption that man is perfectible, but its followers believed that, if children were indeed to become intelligent and virtuous adults, both knowledge and sound moral values had to be impressed upon them at an early age and that this could be done subtly and painlessly through the medium of fiction. Shillaber, who was well acquainted with contemporary moralistic and didactic fiction for boys, created Ike Partington not merely as a contrast to the priggish and unnatural heroes of this fiction but, more importantly, as a satirical weapon to attack the didactic school and the genteel and false values which it promulgated. Ike, who is a realistic rather than a model boy, lies, steals, fights, plays hookey, and plagues people with his practical jokes; but Shillaber does not use his behavior as an excuse to moralize. Instead, in his portrait of Ike he affirms not only his faith in the innate goodness of mankind but also his firm belief that, given love, a good example, and a loose rein, a boy will in time mature into a decent and psychologically healthy man without the help of Sunday-school books and the shallow concept of morality which they espoused.

In addition to his artistic purpose of satirizing moral and didactic tales for boys, then, Shillaber obviously had in mind the more practical aim of attemping to inculcate in adults an attitude toward children which had more in common with that of Rousseau or John Dewey than that assumed by the didactic school. In Shillaber's discussion of Ike in "Experiences During Many Years," he explains that he conceived of Ike as an "imitation of the universal human boy" and that coming to terms with such a boy calls for "a wisdom, patience, and forbearance that might have taxed even Solomon himself." [3]

In "Bringing up Children," an earlier essay, Shillaber ironically outlines some of the practices which parents should follow in rearing children. Parents, he says, should continually whip and scold their offspring, refuse to counsel them, spurn their affections, show them no love, and fail to praise them for their accomplishments. He concludes: "The interests of time and eternity depend upon judicious family training; and yet how few there are who know how to bring up children in the way they should go." [4] Mrs. Partington, who is patient and permissive rather than stern and authoritarian in her relationship with Ike, seems to demonstrate the practical application of Shillaber's theory of child rearing; and her tolerance, benevolence, and vernacular sense of values set a good example for the boy. Mrs. Partington expresses her own common-sense attitude toward Ike as follows:

"He's so full of life and animosity. . . . But there isn't no malice in him, and when he fastened old Mr. Blaze into his own house so that he couldn't get out to drive the boys away from coasting in his field, it wasn't ugliness, though Mr. Blaze said he'd never live till he died because he did it. Depend upon it them boys isn't the worse for being a little mischievous and mark it when you will," continued she, raising her finger till it closed perpendicular as a lightning rod, "the stillest boys isn't always the best—the still sow eats the swill—and some boys who have always had great influenzas, never profits by them when they get so they can act out themselves. For my part I'd rather see boy or man show himself right out at the beginning than find him a boy constructor at last that I have been warming in my bosom to sting it." [5]

Ike, who is seldom open or forthright in his mischievousness, continually tests Mrs. Partington's patience in many varied and imaginative ways. Playing practical jokes on his aunt is one of the most common forms which his mischief-making takes. In "Paul's Ghost," for example, he dresses in the uniform of his deceased Uncle Paul and rather heartlessly convinces his aunt, who has recently read and heard much about the popular cult of spiritualism, that he is her dead husband's ghost:

It was just in the nigh edge of a summer evening, and Mrs. Partington, who had worked hard at her knitting all day, began to feel a little dozy. She felt, as she described it to her neighbor, Mrs. Battlegash, "a sort of alloverness;" and those who have felt as she thus described it, will know the precise sensation;—for ourselves, never having felt so, we cannot explain it.

It was a sort of half twilight, when the daylight begins to be thick and muddy, and a time when ghosts are said to be round fully as plenty as at the classic hour of midnight. We never could see the propriety of restricting ghostly operations to this sombre hour, and, as far as our experience goes, we have seen as many ghosts at "noon of day" as at the "noon of night."

She never told us why, or if she were thinking of ghosts at this time; indeed, all we know about the ghost was from Mrs. Battlegash, and we shall have to give the narration as we had it under Mrs. B.'s own hand:—

"Says Mrs. Part'nton, says she, 'Mrs. Battle,' she always calls me Battle, though my name is Battlegash—my husband's name, and his father's—says she, 'Mrs. Battle, I've seen an apprehension;' and I thought she was agoing to have an asterisk, she was so very pale and haggard like; and says I, 'What's the matter?' for I felt kind of skeered. I had heered a good deal bout the spirituous manifestations, and didn't know but they had been a manifesting her. Says I, 'What's the matter,' agin, and then says she, as solum as a graveyard, 'I've seen Paul!' I felt cold chills a crawlin all over me, but I mustard courage enough to say, 'Do tell!' 'Yes,' says she, 'I saw him with my mortal eyes, just as he looked when he was a tenement of clay, with the very soger clo'es and impertinences he had on the last day he sarved his country in the auxillary.'

"I tried to comfort the poor cretur by telling her that I guessed he didn't keer enough about her to want to come back, and as his estate had all been settled sacreligiously, it would be very unreasonable indeed in him to come back to disturb her.

"'Where did you see him?' says I. 'Out into the yard,' said she. 'When did you see him?' says I. 'Just now,' said she. 'Are you shore it was he?' said I, determined to get at the bottom of it. 'Yes,' said she, 'if ever an apprehension did come back, that 'ere was one. P'raps it is there now.' Then says I, 'Ruth,' says I, 'le's go and see.'

"She riz right up, and we walked along through the long entry into her room, and looked out of her back window, and there, shore enough, was a sight as froze my blood to calves-foot jelly. There was the soger cap and coat, as nateral as life, with the tompion atop. My heart come up into my mouth, so that I could have spit it out just as easy as not. Mrs. Part'nton, says she, 'What do you think of it? isn't it his apprehension? But I'm determined to speak to it.'

"I tried to persuade her not to, but she insisted on it, and out she went.

" 'Paul! ' said she, 'what upon airth do you want, that you should come back arter it, so apprehensively? ' The figure was setting on the top of the pump when she spoke, and it didn't take no notice of her. 'Paul! ' said she, a little louder. Then slowly and solemly that 'ere cap turned round, and instead of Paul, Mr. Editor, if you'll believe it, it was Ike, the little scapegrace, that had frightened us almost out of our wits, if we ever had any. That boy, I believe, will be the means of somebody's death. Mrs. Part'nton grew very red in the face, and razed her hand to inflict corporal punishment onto the young corporal, but the boy looked up kind of pleasantly like, and she couldn't find the heart to strike him, though I told her if she spared the rod she would spile that 'ere child. It is fortnight for him that he isn't a child of mine, I can tell him."

Here Mrs. Battlegash's narrative ends. We can fancy the scene in the yard: the youngster in the corporal's coat, the red face changing to pleasant equanimity, the raised hand, indicative of temper, subsiding, as the waves do when the wind ceases to blow, and peace, like the evening star above them, pervading and giving grace to the tableau.[6]

In "Mrs. Partington Ruralizing," the prank which Ike plays on his aunt backfires, and his merriment ends in tears:

Mrs. Partington and Ike were huckleberrying in the country, and a large swamp was wearily canvassed to find the quart which she bore in her five-quart pail. She despaired of filling it.

"Look here, aunt," said Ike, in a sort of confidential whisper, "look in there and see what a lot of 'em."

There was a smile upon the face of the boy, that betokened mischief, or it might have been a gleam of satisfaction at the prospect of filling the pail; but certainly a smile was round the little mouth, and the eye caught it, and a roguish twinkle like a sunbeam lay sparkling there.

"I see! " said the old lady, and a moment later the log-cabin bonnet, borrowed for the occasion, was seen above the tops of the bushes, its restlessness indicating its wearer's activity. Ike remained outside.

Fizz-z-z—Buzz-z-z! —what was that? —a humble-bee, as we are a sinner. Another and another. The log cabin was besieged, and Mrs. Partington rushed frantically from the bushes, swinging the tin pail and crying "Shoo! shoo! " with all her might. It was a trying time for the widow of Corporal Paul. And Ike did not escape, for a big humblebee attacked him, and he roared heartily with a sting upon his cheek. The laugh disappeared.

At the recital of their troubles at home, people regarded the matter as a trick of Ike's; but how could he have known about the humblebee's nest being in there? Mrs. Partington avowed that she "never was so frustrated by anything in her born days," and the people believed her. She thinks, notwithstanding the bees, that she would like to have a "villain" in the country, and become an "amatory" farmer.[7]

In "A Prediction," Ike plagues his aunt rather cruelly by rushing into the house shouting, "O aunt, I just now saw a little boy fall down under a sleigh in Washington-street! " When his aunt, horror-stricken, asks him if the boy was killed, Ike replies, "O, no aunt . . . it didn't hurt him at all, for the sleigh hadn't any horse in it." [8]

Sometimes Ike teases his aunt in true boyish fashion by deliberately misinterpreting her remarks:

"You never see sich chaney no ware now, as this," said Mrs. Partington, as she took from an obscure corner of the old cupboard a teapot of antique appearance, noseless and handleless, and cracked here and there, and stayed with putty where Time's mischievous fingers had threatened a dissolution of the union. "That teapot was my grand-mother's afore she was married; I remember it just as well as it was yesterday."

"Remember when your grandmother was married? " queried Ike.

"No, no, the teapot," responded she; "and it was a perfect beauty, with the Garden of Eden on it, and the flowers and Adam and Eve on it, so natural that you might almost smell their fragrance."

"What, smell Adam and Eve? " said Ike.

"No, the flowers, stupid! " replied she; "my grand-'ther gave it to her as a memento mori of his undying infection, because the colors wouldn't fade, and they never have, though children are destroying angels, and they made the mischief among the crockery, as they always do now-a-days."

She had held the teapot in her hands as she spoke, and now she gazed in silence upon the picture of Adam and Eve, partially concealed in the bushes, and she revelled in the memory of the past, and wondered if her grandmother ever came back to look at that old teapot that she had preserved so carefully, as an heir-loom; then, carefully brushing off some dust that rested upon it, she replaced it, and charged Ike impressively to keep it most sacrilegiously for her sake. He said he would, as plain as his mouth full of preserved plums would let him, and wiped his mouth on the sleeve of his best jacket.[9]

When Ike wearies of teasing and tormenting his aunt, he never hesitates to look further afield for an unsuspecting victim. In an anecdote entitled "Fourth of July," he plays a dangerous practical joke on a complete stranger:

"Isaac! " said Mrs. Partington, rapping on the window, as she saw the boy in the act of putting half a bunch of crackers into the pocket of a countryman who stood viewing the procession. The caution came too late, and the individual was astonished! Isaac had stepped inside the door to await the explosion, and the old lady met him in the entry. "O, you spirit of mischief! " cried she, "what will become of you if you go on in this way? Is this all your idees of liberty and regeneration, that you must fill that poor man's pockets with your crackers? Do you suppose this was all that the days of 7 by 6 was made for? I should think you would be ashamed to look upon your Uncle Paul's picter there, and hide your face in conclusion, arter behaving so! Ah! " she mused, "how different boys are now from what they used to be!—so wild, so rakeless and tricky"—(crack!)—"what's that? I should like to know who fired that. It was a great piece of impudence"—(crack!)—"goodness gracious! somebody must be throwin' 'em into the windows." She ran to look out. Not a soul was near that could have done it. Crack! another explosion at her feet, and she looked round. Isaac sat demurely eating some gingerbread by the table, but said nothing. There was an expression about his mouth which looked torpedoish, and for a moment she mistrusted him; but he couldn't have done it, he was so quiet, and she shut the window that opened upon the street, to prevent their throwing in any more.[10]

Like most boys, Ike is attracted to animals, and many of the anecdotes relate his experiences with members of the animal kingdom. In an amusing and realistic monologue entitled "Ike and the Elephant," he visits the zoo; and, while he is admiring the elephant, the beast steals his gingerbread. Both frightened and angry, Ike talks belligerently to the elephant in true boylike fashion:

I s'pose you think you've done thunderin' great things, don't you? For my part, I don't call it no better'n stealing. O, you may stand there and swing that trunk of yourn just as much as you're a mind to; you can't skeer a fellow, I tell *you*! This is a free country, old club-feet; and you a'nt agoing to take any more liberties here like that. I can tell you it won't be safe for that old Ingee-rubber hide o' yourn, if you do! you take my gingerbread away, agin, if you dare, that's all. You just try it, you ongainly reptile, you.[11]

Ike has a dog named Lion of which he is fond but which he also sometimes annoys unmercifully. In "Ike and Lion," he teases his aunt and makes Lion miserable by dressing the animal in a coffee bag and tying one of Mrs. Partington's nightcaps on his head. In consternation his aunt says, "Dear me . . . I'm afraid your predestination will not be a good one, if you go on so; and little boys who tease their aunts don't go to heaven, by a great sight." [1 2]

Ike's favorite diversion, however, seems to be badgering cats; and sometimes his treatment of them reveals a streak of childish cruelty in him. In "Ike in the Country," he goes to the country on a winter day to visit some of Mrs. Partington's relatives. After he becomes bored with snowballing cattle, catching hens in a box trap, and tying pigs together, he decides to amuse himself by annoying the cat:

Ike had watched this cat wistfully ever since he had been there, and the cat had mainfested a strange repugnance to him ever since he trod on her tail as she lay by the stove. He immediately seized upon her, and expedients, never wanting, soon suggested themselves to him.

There were plenty of clam-shells about the yard, and, selecting four of the smoothest, he, by the aid of some grafting wax at hand, soon had Tabby beautifully shod with clam-shells and on the way to the river. Ike's idea was to learn her to skate!

The river was smooth as glass, and a sharp wind blew along its surface towards the bay. "Now, Puss," said Ike, as he pushed her upon the ice, "go it! " An instinct of danger instantly seized upon her. Her claws, which Ike had found so sharp a short time before, were now useless to her, and, with a growl of spite, she swelled her caudal appendage to an enormous size which, taking the wind, impelled the poor feline like a clipper over the slippery path. The tail stood straight as a topmast, and grew bigger and bigger, and faster and faster flew the animal to which the tail belonged. Ike laughed till he cried to see the cat scudding before the wind. But now the bay lay before her, and far out over the smooth ice was the blue water of the sea.

The result can be guessed. The cat never came back, and everybody wondered what had become of her, and thought it augured ill luck for a cat to leave a house so suddenly. Ike thought so, especially for the cat.

Ike's conscience reproached him sadly, but he compromised the matter by leaving the tenants of the barnyard in peace all the while he staid there, and came home with a pocket full of doughnuts and an enviable reputation for propriety. [1 3]

In "How Ike Dropped the Cat," however, he goes beyond the bounds of mere mischief in his treatment of another cat. In this anecdote, Mrs. Partington, who is weary of the antics of her cat, requests Ike to "take our Tabby and drop her somewhere, and see that she don't come back again. . . ." Ike dutifully sets off with the cat; and, when he returns, his aunt questions him: "Did she drop easy, Isaac . . . and won't she come back again? " After Ike has assured her that the cat dropped "easy" and will not return, she glances out of the window and sees the cat dangling from an apple tree. Ike earnestly assures her that the cat was so despondent over being rejected that she committed suicide by hanging herself; and his aunt accepts his far-fetched explanation.[14]

Like Tom Sawyer, Ike is an expert in devising ways to deceive his aunt; and, because of her kindness and naïveté, he usually succeeds. The following illustrates one of the stratagems which he employs to hoodwink her:

"There, don't take on so, dear," said Mrs. Partington, as she handed Ike a peach he had been crying for. He took the peach, and a minute afterwards was heard whistling "Jordon" on the ridgepole of the shed. "He is sich a tender-hearted critter," said she to Mrs. Sled, smilingly, while that excellent neighbor looked at him through the window with two deprecatory eyes—"He is so tender-hearted that I can't ask him to go out and draw an armful of wood or split a pail of water without setting him crying at once." [15]

Like Tom Sawyer, too, Ike enjoys playing pirate and acting out hair-raising episodes from Edward Carroll Judson's *The Black Avenger of the Spanish Main; or, The Fiend of Blood: A Thrilling Tale of Buccaneer Times by Ned Buntline;*[16] and this wild and boisterous kind of play is a vexation to his aunt:

"Ha! ha! Down with the tyrant! Death to the Spaniard! " shouted Ike, as he rushed into the kitchen, brandishing Paul's old artillery sword that had hung so long on the wall. He struck an attitude, and then struck the upright portion of the stove funnel till it rung with the blow, and Mrs. Partington, with amazement on her countenance and the glass lamp in her hand, stood looking at him. Ike had been reading the thrilling tale of the "Black Avenger, or the Pirate of the Spanish Main," and his "intellects," as Sir Hugh Evans might say, were absorbed by the horrible.

"Don't, Isaac, dear," said Mrs. Partington, and she spoke in a gentle, but firm tone. "You are very scarifying, and it don't look well to see a young boy acting so. It comes, I know, of reading them yellow cupboard books. You should read good ones; and if you won't touch that again I will let you have my big Bible, king James's aversion, with the beautiful pictures. I declare, I don't know what I shall do with you if you carry on so. I am afraid I shall have to send you to a geological cemetery to get the old sancho out of you."

The point of the sword was lowered as it was making a passage for a dark spot in the centre panel of the door; the eye of the boy, so fiercely lit by the spirit ot the "Black Avenger," became mild and laughing, as he said he was only "making b'lieve," and Mrs. Partington gave him a penny as she disarmed him. What a visible emotion of peanuts became manifest as he grasped the copper and made tracks for the door, and climbed over the snow drifts to reach the grocer's opposite! [17]

In spite of her stern Calvinistic upbringing, Mrs. Partington is neither narrow nor dogmatic in her religious views; and, although she sends Ike to church, she does not attempt to force an unnatural piety on him as the authors of the Sunday-school books essayed to urge it upon their youthful readers:

"Now go to meeting, dear," said Mrs. Partington, as Isaac stood smoothing his hair preparatory to going out on Sunday. He looked down at his new shoes, and a thought of the green fields made him sigh. A fishing line hung out of one pocket, which Mrs. Partington didn't see.

"Where shall I go to? " asked Ike.

Since the old lady had given up her seat in the Old North church, she had no stated place of worship.

"Go," replied she sublimely, as she pulled down his jacket behind, "go anywheres where the gospel is dispensed with." [18]

Ike, like Tom Sawyer, has an aversion to attending church, and he finds it impossible to behave during services. In "Ike at Church," he refuses to listen to the sermon, he lowers a pencil on a string over the gallery onto the head of a boy below, and he draws a picture on the cover of a new hymnal. His aunt lectures him severely but with little effect:

"You have been acting very bad in meeting," continued she, "and I could hardly keep from boxing your ears right in the middle of the lethargy. You don't pay no interest, and I lost all the thread of the sermon through your tricks"—"I didn't take your thread," said Ike, who thought she alluded to the string by which the pencil was lowered upon the boy; "that was a fishing line."—"O, Isaac," continued she earnestly, "what do you want to act like the probable son, for? Why don't you try and be like David and Deuteronomy, that we read about, and act in a reprehensible manner? "[19]

Although Mrs. Partington does not attempt to make of Ike a pious boy, she does feel it her duty to counsel him against conduct not in accord with the middle-class code. Her good intentions come to naught, however, because her homilies inevitably dissolve in comic confusion. In "Wholesome Advice," for example, she lectures him earnestly and ineffectively on the subject of gambling:

"Isaac," said Mrs. Partington, as that interesting juvenile was playing a game of "knuckle up" against the kitchen wall, to the imminent danger of the old clock which ticked near by, "this is a marvellous age, as Deacon Babson says, and perhaps there's no harm in 'em, but I'm afeard no good'll come out of it—no good at all—for you to keep playing marvels all the time, as you do. I am afeard you will learn how to gambol, and become a bad boy, and forget all the good device I have given you. Ah! it would break my soul, Isaac, to have you given to naughty tricks, like some wicked boys that I know, who will be rakeshames in the airth if they don't die before their time comes. So, don't gambol, dear, and always play as if you had just as lieves the minister would see you as not." She handed him a little bag she had made for him to keep his marbles in, and patted his head kindly as he went again to play. Ike was fortified, for the next five minutes, against temptation to do evil; but

> "Chase span, in the ring,
> Knuckle up, or anything,"

are potent when arrayed against out-of-sight solicitude, and we fear that the boy forgot. There is much reason in the old lady's fear.[20]

Because of his incessant mischievousness, Ike is a constant worry and vexation to Mrs. Partington, but she cannot bring herself to be authoritarian. In "Mrs. Partington on Vacation," she looks forward to the closing of school with dread and anxiety although she knows that Ike needs a vacation:

"Five weeks' vexation in August! " said Mrs. Partington, when she heard that the school had a vacation for five weeks; "five weeks' vexation! " It is a trying season for mothers, and wearing and tearing to their patience and the jackets and trousers of their children. Talk about relaxing from study! I don't believe it is half as bad as the green apples they get in the country. But I do love to see the little dears enjoying themselves, frisking about like pigs in clover, as happy as the days is long. What an idea of freedom there is in a little boy with his face and hair full of molasses and fun and good nature! "Be still, you good-for-nothing! " cried she, as Ike attempted to take her snuff-box; "Be still, I say! " [21]

Mrs. Partington, in "The Guardian for Ike," finally becomes so exasperated with Ike that she comes to the conclusion that a guardian must be appointed to assist her in rearing him. After considerable thought, she settles on her friend Old Roger as the most likely candidate for the task, and she invites him and several other friends to her home to discuss the matter. After Ike misdirects Old Roger to the Partington home, the elderly gentleman is not enthusiastic about the assignment; but when he discovers that Ike has defended a lame boy against the brutal onslaught of a gang of bullies and has also given him a dime which Old Roger himself had given Ike, he comes to the conclusion that Ike is basically a good boy and forgives him for his peccadilloes:

A boy that doesn't have fun isn't always to be trusted; and the one who has his wits about him, and does not take to fun, will, depend upon it, take to something worse. Parents mistake when they put an unyielding check upon a boy's conduct; when he gets his way, he will, nine times in ten, go differently from his direction, and covert sin will work insidiously, maugre all interdiction. I can't bear to see a parchment-faced boy, with a ledger in his glance at ten. Give me the lad with his soul speaking in his laughing eye, and thrilling in every nerve of his animated body. This is your true boyhood. Where there is no malice, mischief is not sin. . . . [22]

It is clear from his portrayal of Ike Partington that, although Shillaber was not a sentimentalist, he did believe that true virtue is a matter of the heart rather than a result of conformity to a prescribed code of behavior. It is clear, too, that he believed that, although children can be exasperating, it is far better to allow them to grow up free and naturally than to attempt to make them miniature adults by forcing genteel language and manners upon them. Ike Partington, despite his mischievousness and thoughtlessness, is basically good and unspoiled and in time will presumably mature into a responsible and humane adult.

Because Shillaber was one of the most severe, persistent, and effective critics of the didacticism and sterility of contemporary juvenile fiction during the two decades between 1848 and 1868, he deserves recognition as one of the forces behind the renaissance in children's literature which began in the late 1860's. But, probably because Ike Partington has long been forgotten and because Shillaber wrote no classic in the field, he has not received that recognition. Even specialists in the study of children's literature today seem generally ignorant of Shillaber and his efforts to improve writing for children. The humor, the realism, and the vitality which he promoted through Ike Partington appeared in some measure in 1868 in Louisa May Alcott's *Little Women* and in Thomas Bailey Aldrich's *Story of a Bad Boy*. It appeared in full measure in 1876 in Mark Twain's *The Adventures of Tom Sawyer,* probably the best and most popular book for young readers ever written by an American writer. Although it cannot be demonstrated that Shillaber was a direct influence on these three writers, it is evident that he helped to create a literary climate favorable to their fiction.

II   *Books for Boys*

In addition to the periodical pieces in which Ike Partington appears, Shillaber wrote and published three books for boys in which Ike plays at least a minor role: *Ike Partington; or, The Adventures of a Human Boy and His Friends* (1879); *Cruises with Captain Bob on Sea and Land* (1880); and *The Double-Runner Club; or, the Lively Boys of Riverton* (1882). Attractively printed, illustrated and bound, all three books were published by Lee and Shepard, a firm which published juvenile fiction by such popular authors as William Taylor Adams, author of the Oliver Optic series; Elijah Kellogg, author of the Elm Island and Pleasant Cove series; and Rebecca Clark, who wrote the Little Prudy and Dotty Dimple books for girls.

Ike Partington and His Friends, the first of Shillaber's books for boys, although not an unqualified success, is the best of the series. The book, which is not didactic in nature, relates from a third-person point of view the experiences of Ike Partington during one year of his life. Ike's experiences, which are not of a dime-novel variety, are probably typical of those of a nineteenth-century New England boy; and they are certainly based in part, at least, on Shillaber's boyhood experiences in Portsmouth, New Hampshire. In his preface to the book, Shillaber says that he is attempting to present Ike as a representative and realistic boy inhabiting a typical boy's world:

The Boy must not be judged by the standard of Childhood or Manhood. He has a sphere of his own; and all of his mischief, frolic, and general deucedness belong to his own condition. The Boy has but little plan, purpose, or intention, in what he does, beyond having a good time. Boys that think, and have no interest in the doings of boyhood, may be delightful aids to a quiet home; but the life, spirit, energy, and health of the active Boy, come with his activity. As for boyish fun, it is not so much that as it is experiment; and the boyish reader of these pages will see how it is for himself.[23]

Unlike Twain in *The Adventures of Tom Sawyer,* Shillaber does not present the boy's world as a violent one, nor does he explore the terrible fears which can torment children. There are no murders, grave robberies, or lost children in the book; and there is no villain to match Injun Joe. Unlike the world which Tom inhabits on the Missouri frontier, Ike's world is generally stable, secure, and peaceful; and, perhaps as a result, *Ike Partington* is a much less exciting book than *Tom Sawyer.*

Thematically, the book is loosely structured around Ike's slow, faltering progress from the selfishness and irresponsibility of childhood toward the altruism and responsibility of adulthood. The narrative structure is episodic, and incident follows incident with few causal relationships among them. What unity the work possesses results from the fact that Ike is the central character and that his maturing is the central theme of the book. Although Mrs. Partington is a character in the book, she plays a very minor role in it.

When the book opens, Mrs. Partington has decided that, because of the poor state of Ike's health, she and her nephew will move to Clam Corner, a suburb of the city of Riverton. Riverton, which is located on the seacoast of New England, is almost certainly modeled on Shillaber's native city of Portsmouth. After Ike and his aunt are settled in Clam Corner, he enters a school taught by a man who is a very strict disciplinarian. Although Ike is as mischievous at school as at home, he is also shrewd, and he generally manages to outwit the schoolmaster. Ike makes friends with his schoolmates and with Captain Bob Davit, a retired sailor who enjoys the companionship of children. The creek or river upon which Clam Corner is located provides Ike and his friends many opportunities for adventure. They build an oven for baking clams, which are extremely plentiful in the area; they catch an enormous monk fish which they proudly put on exhibit in town; they cruise on the river on the *Jolly Roger,* Captain Bob's boat; they have a narrow escape when the boat capsizes and dumps them into the stream.

One of the longer episodes in the book relates Ike's experiences during the two weeks which he spends on a farm belonging to the uncle of one of Ike's friends, Sim Walters. Although Ike finds no pleasure in making hay or in hoeing corn, he does enjoy fishing in the river and playing in the woods with Sim. He and Sim stir up a hornets' nest, attempt to drown a woodchuck out of his hole, and make a "Hail Columbia" bird of a rooster by painting him red, white, and blue.

Back in Clam Corner following his stay in the country, Ike is confined to the house for several weeks after he injures his wrists by falling from a tree. During the boredom of his confinement, he teases the cat and visits with Mark Treddle, an elderly eccentric who imagines that he converses with the prophet Jeremiah and other biblical characters. After Ike recovers and winter comes on, the boys skate on the ice, go sledding, have snowball fights, and tell stories. It is on a cold winter day that a small boy walks onto the thin ice of the river, sinks into the river, and drowns, despite the frantic efforts of Captain Bob and the older boys to save him. The drowning incident is Shillaber's sole attempt at *frisson;* he makes no further effort in the book to provoke horror in the reader. As spring approaches the river begins to melt, and the boys amuse themselves by engaging in the dangerous sport of riding cakes of ice down the river. The book ends with the boys returning to their old haunts in the fields, the woods, and the river bank.

The book has many good qualities. Ike is a fairly convincing character who is presented as a "human" rather than as a model boy in the didactic tradition. Ike is also a developing character who matures in his relationships both with his peers and with grownups, and the maturation theme is neither obtrusive nor offensive. In spite of its strengths, however, the work as a whole fails as a boy's book; consequently, it has not survived. The main reason for its failure is not difficult to discover. It is true that it tells no coherent story, that its various episodes are not highly dramatic, and that it lacks the compression and stylistic excellence of the earlier anecdotes featuring Ike, but none of these characteristics is the cause of the book's failure.

The basic flaw is that Shillaber loses sight of his audience and directs the book toward adult rather than juvenile readers. The book does not, like *Tom Sawyer,* re-create imaginatively the unique world of boyhood from a boy's point of view; instead, it pictures boys acting out reminiscences of Shillaber's own boyhood. The concluding paragraph of the book shows conclusively that he has lost sight of his audience altogether: "Thus a single year of a boy's life rounded to its close, with its joys, failures, accidents, mischiefs, companionships, and trials,—the ups and downs of the journey towards manhood. Ike Partington is a fair representative of his entire class. His is no phenomenal or exceptional case; and in his adventures and those of his friends are found the same characteristics that distinguish the human boy all round the world and will become the grandest manhood." [24] The results of Shillaber's failure to keep his audience in mind are a condescending tone, a blurring of the effect of the book, and an understandable confusion on the part of the reader, child or adult, as he is torn between the worlds of boyhood and manhood.

Cruises With Captain Bob, the second of Shillaber's series for boys, differs in several respects from *Ike Partington.* First, it is a travel book in the tradition of Abbott's Little Rollo books; second, it is constructed around Captain Bob Davit, with Ike and his friends becoming mere listeners and questioners. The plan of the book is simple. Because Captain Davit breaks his leg, he is immobilized for several weeks during the winter; and, being bored and lonely, he agrees to tell the boys each evening a story of his experiences at sea and in faraway places. Although the book as a whole is presented from a third-person point of view, the travel stories are told in first person by the captain. The book, which has no central theme, was undoubtedly designed to be both informative and entertaining, but it is interesting today only to the student of Shillaber, and it is of interest to him chiefly because of its autobiographical content.

Following an introduction by the author, the Captain, who is a very bland character for an ex-sailor, launches on his storytelling venture. After relating a few preliminary stories about some of his early experiences aboard ship, he commences his main yarn, which concerns a voyage to Demerara, British Guiana, and his stay in that South American country. This long narrative, Shillaber explains in his preface to the book, is based on his own experience in 1836—38 when poor health forced him to live in Demerara. [25]

Forged in an undistinguished colloquial style, the Captain's story, which is continued from night to night, falls into three parts: his voyage to Demerara, his sojourn there, and his voyage back home. He tells of his departure on a winter's day from Hartford, Connecticut, aboard the brig *Alexander,* which carried both passengers and a cargo of horses. After narrating his experiences on the voyage to Demerara and his arrival there, he tells how he became ill and was forced to spend several months in that city. Then, in the manner of the Little Rollo books, he reports on the geography, the people, the social customs, and the flora and fauna of the country. He describes a tropical rainstorm; explains the process of making sugar; tells about the raising of pineapples, bananas, and coconuts; and describes burial customs, Easter parades, and masquerade parties. He also digresses on such miscellaneous subjects as deep-sea fishing, pirates, and history. Finally, after the Captain narrates the events of the voyage home, the book closes with Ike and his friends waiting for the coming of spring in Riverton. A dull and didactic book, it fails chiefly because it is presented in a patronizing tone and from an adult point of view.

The Double Runner Club, Shillaber's third and last book for boys, is unquestionably the poorest of the series. Constructed of a hodge-podge of anecdotes, tales, and verse held loosely together by a framework, the book is structurally weak, and its subject matter is dull. The framework itself is clumsy and contrived. Ike and his friends organize a club for the purpose of making a double-runner sled. After completing the sled, they decide to continue the club and to meet throughout the winter months in Captain Bob's boathouse for sessions of reading and storytelling. The book has no plot and portrays no full-bodied characters. Although Shillaber states in his preface that "The aim of the book is to show that boys, governed by rules of their own imposing, can do as well as those of older growth, and to illustrate the possibility of continued youth, as shown by the genial veteran, 'Captain Bob,' in his kindly intercourse with the boys," [26] his chief interest in the book seems to be in the miscellaneous anecdotes, tales, and verse which the boys tell and read.

The story and verse contained within the structural frame of the book represent a wide variety of subjects and moods. Some of the pieces hinge on humor, some on suspense, some on didacticism, some on sentiment, and several on patriotism. "Burglars in the House," for example, is a humorous story about a series of blunders on the part of two neighbors, each of whom mistakes the other for a burglar. [27] "The Black Fairy" is a suspenseful story of two boys who become lost in a forest during a snowstorm and are rescued by a dog. [28] "Do Something" is a didactic story about a lazy boy from a wealthy family who spends a vacation in the country where he meets a poor crippled boy who convinces him of the value of work. [29] "Captain Bob's Story" is a sentimental tale about a ne'er-do-well minister's son who leaves home and then returns years later to his sorrowing family laden with wealth and rescues them from poverty.[30] Patriotism is the theme of verses written by Ike Partington and read by him on Washington's birthday.[31] Despite the great variety of forms and subjects included in it, the book fails because almost without exception the material is trite and dull and because, like the other two books in the series, it is presented from the viewpoint of an adult.

Shillaber's books for boys are not artistically successful because he lacked Twain's ability to translate satire of didactic and moralistic tales into the form and substance of artistic fiction for boys themselves to enjoy. The writer of enduring books for children must possess both the imagination to see life as a child sees it and the literary skill to present experience in a language which speaks to children. Without doubt Shillaber loved, respected, and understood children and sympathized with them in their resistance to authoritarianism; but he failed as a writer of juvenile fiction because he was unable to assume the child's point of view. Although he could convey to adults his perceptive insights into the nature and behavior of children, he lacked the imagination to see as a child, feel as a child, and be as a child; as a result, his books are nearly as self-conscious and condescending as those which he was attacking. Shillaber effectively satirized the artistic and moral values of the didactic school of writers, but in his own books for boys he did not succeed in providing an antidote to their corrupting influence.

CHAPTER 5

Popular Fiction and Verse

BENJAMIN Penhallow Shillaber was an amazingly versatile and voluminous writer. In addition to humorous and satirical pieces, travel sketches, feature articles, and news stories, he wrote a great quantity of verse and fiction to fill the pages of the newspapers and magazines with which he was connected as a staff member or as an editor. Except for what Shillaber himself collected in his books, his verse and fiction have not been collected and probably never will be; for although they are competently written, they lack the literary merit of his best humor. Aware that he was not writing for posterity, he deliberately and skillfully shaped his verse and fiction to please and entertain his audience. Shrewdly gauging the tastes of popular readers, he used the subjects which they enjoyed, he employed the formulas to which they were conditioned, and he endorsed the values which they accepted. Indeed, a careful analysis of his popular verse and fiction reveals much more concerning contemporary popular taste than it does about Shillaber's abilities as a literary artist.

I *Fiction*

Shillaber published no novels, but he did publish several novelettes and numerous pieces of short fiction, many of which appeared in the *Saturday Evening Gazette.* Just how much magazine and newspaper fiction he published as a free-lance writer after he left the *Gazette,* there is no way of knowing, but it may have been a considerable amount. His fiction, for the most part, can most accurately be classified as popular romance. Although some of his stories contain elements of burlesque, most of them are neither humorous nor satirical, and none of them has the pungency or the originality of his best humor. In his fiction Shillaber is satisfied to try for surface effects only, and he usually depends upon plot and situation rather than upon theme and characterization for his effects. He employs stock characters, and he pays very little attention to setting. In the tradition of stage melodrama, he arranges incidents to lead his readers from one stock emotional response to another with almost no regard for convincing motivation. He also uses coincidence, sentimentality, suspense, mystery, intrigue, mistaken identity, and many of the other standard contrivances of the popular romance. Intent upon entertaining, he generally does not moralize nor concern himself with serious ideas of any kind. His style, which is competent but undistinguished, follows the florid and trite stylistic conventions of popular fiction.

Although Shillaber added elements of his own invention, the basic situations and plots which he utilized in his romances were generally ones which had been popularized by writers of fiction and stage melodrama. Romantic love stories were popular then as now, and most of Shillaber's plots are constructed around a love interest. "A Life's Fortunes," for example, is a story of thwarted love with a happy ending. James Trevor, the hero of the story, is a farmer's son who is indentured to Mr. Edes, a storekeeper. A widower, Mr. Edes has a daughter named Julie who is being reared by a very strict aunt also named Julie Edes. After falling in love, the two young people meet secretly until Aunt Julie intercepts a letter from Trevor to her niece arranging a tryst and exposes them to the girl's father. In narrating this sad turn of events, Shillaber moves toward burlesque when, with tongue in cheek, he reminds the reader that, in using the device of the purloined letter, he is simply following one of the conventions of the popular romance:

Alas! that I must dash this beautiful scene to pieces, and strew salt upon its ground, so that nothing shall grow there more! But I am truthful in my narration, and a reputation achieved by a long life of veracity must not be endangered by any wrong statement. A letter—O, that lovers should ever know how to write! O, that they knew how to avoid ink! O, that they would write their tender missives in paregoric or water!—directed to "Julie Edes," appointing a meeting on the balcony, fell into the hands of the the aunt, instead of the daughter.[1]

Mr. Edes, of course, dismisses Trevor, who, after leaving a letter in which he promises to return and marry Julie, steals a large sum of money from his employer and disappears. Julie, who does not receive the letter, suffers a long illness but finally recovers. Trevor travels to Haiti where he makes and loses a fortune and then to Marseilles where he marries and makes another fortune. Meanwhile, Julie's father and aunt die; the aunt confesses on her deathbed that she purloined Trevor's letter to Julie. Trevor loses his money, his wife deserts him, and he sets out for the United States; but on the voyage home he has the misfortune to come down with a fever.

When the ship docks, Julie, who is helping to care for the sick travelers and who does not recognize him, takes him to her home to care for him. She finally does recognize him; he recovers; and, since he is still legally married and "the hey day of their blood has grown tame," they live happily together in a platonic relationship. Although Shillaber gives a slightly new twist to the resolution—the plot constructed around thwarted love—the purloined letter, the mistaken identity, the unsympathetic aunt, the faithful female lover, the strained coincidences, and the hero's running away and making his fortune are all well-worn devices of popular fiction and melodrama.

"Missing" is another love story with a very complex and sensational plot in which an incestuous marriage is narrowly avoided. The story begins with the mysterious disappearance of George Wayne, a successful farmer, who leaves a wife and two sons. The mother remarries; the boys grow up; and, after a number of years, she becomes a widow again. Of the two sons, Harry remains on the farm; George goes to the city, where "integrity and industry secured him friends, and his shrewdness and foresight won him position."

In the city, George becomes acquainted with the three daughters of Solon Francis. After informing the reader that the girls' mother is dead, Shillaber skirts the edges of burlesque when he mockingly apologizes for introducing sad incidents into the story but then excuses himself by pointing out that he is merely following the conventions of popular romance: "I am sorry to introduce these mortuary episodes into a cheerful story,—first George Wayne, and then the mother of these charming girls,—but the exigency of the plot demands it. I have, however, done better than most tale-writers, who dismiss the mothers of their stories with but one pale-faced girl, to live in a state of uselessness, and make some spooney fellow 'happy' in the future, for Mrs. Francis left three, and one son, who was a shipmaster, whom George Wayne had not seen." [2]

George eventually becomes engaged to Alice, one of the Francis sisters, but before they marry, his employer asks him to go to France on a business mission with Florinda Willison, the daughter of one of the firm's wine representatives. Florinda's father is suffering from loss of memory and is unable to perform his duties. George falls in love with Florinda, and, as his love for her grows, his love for Alice cools until he breaks his engagement to her. The climactic incident occurs when Mr. Willison sees the couple embracing, his mind providentially and melodramatically clears, and he tells George that he cannot marry Florinda because she is his sister. But after this startling climax, George marries Alice, Mr. and Mrs. Willison are reunited, and the story ends happily.

The plot of "A New Year's Revery" hinges upon the artifice, popular in romance and melodrama, of the vindication of virtue. As the story begins, the narrator chivalrously sets out to find Mary, a childhood sweetheart, who has run away to the city, presumably Boston. When he arrives in the city, he enlists the aid of the police who, after some investigation, inform him that a young woman of Mary's description lives in Cambridge. Intending to see Mary and to persuade her to return to her grieving mother, he arrives at her house just as a fashionably dressed young man is leaving. After a conversation with her, he is convinced from her apparent embarrassment that she is living in sin with the young man. He visits her a second time and implores her to return, but she refuses to listen to his entreaties. When he goes to call upon her for the third time, the house is empty, and Mary is gone.

Three years later while viewing an exhibition of paintings at the Athenaeum, he is surprised to see a portrait of Mary by the painter Duverne. As he thoughtfully studies the portrait, he falls into conversation with an elderly gentleman who informs him that he is Duverne's uncle, that Duverne is his sole heir, and that he is most unhappy with his nephew because he will not agree to marry the rich and beautiful young woman whom he has chosen for him. When the narrator tells the uncle about the liaison between Duverne and Mary, he refuses to believe it, but he promises to investigate the situation. On the next evening the uncle invites Duverne and the narrator to his home where he accuses his nephew of causing the downfall of Mary. Duverne tells him that he had married Mary under a vow of secrecy because he had feared his uncle's displeasure and that Mary had suffered shame and humiliation rather than divulge the secret. In the denouement, virtue is not only vindicated but is also handsomely rewarded when the uncle begs his nephew's forgiveness and reinstates him as his heir. In this story, as in all of his popular romances, Shillaber subordinates theme and character to situation and plot, and he depends heavily for effect upon the device of deliberately withholding information from the reader and then springing it upon him in the conclusion of the story.[3]

In "Christmas Hearths and Hearts," a long love story which first appeared in the *Gazette,* Shillaber employs to good advantage the popular device of the unknown benefactor. The story begins in 1836 when Mr. Milling, a wealthy merchant, is ruined financially by his partner John Upshur, who had secretly speculated with the firm's money in the Eastern Land Bubble. As a result of this business failure, Mr. and Mrs. Milling and their two daughters are reduced to poverty. Of the two daughters, Matilda is twenty years old and beautiful; Lily, the heroine of the story, is "a fair and gentle creature of ten, delicate as a snowdrop and almost as frail." The business is purchased by Eugene Partelot and George Savage, two of Mr. Milling's clerks. Partelot is suave and charming, while Savage is solitary and uncouth. It is rumored that Mr. Milling was a party to the transaction which ruined his business, and he dies of humiliation in typical sentimental fashion with his tearful family gathered around the bed.

After Mr. Milling's death his widow receives an anonymous letter in which the writer offers to pay for Lily's education. Mrs. Milling accepts the offer. Eugene Partelot, who is courting Matilda, implies that he is the unknown benefactor; but the Millings discover that he is not. By comparing specimens of handwriting, Lily makes the discovery that it is George Savage who is helping her, but she keeps this bit of information to herself. She also develops a secret love for the uncouth Mr. Savage. Through the years she develops into a typical sentimental heroine whom Shillaber describes in the ornate and saccharine style which was typical of contemporary popular romance: "Her beautiful form was a marvel of grace, her face was as bright as an angel's, and her mind endowed with qualities that placed her far before those of her own age and condition. All loved her for her virtues; but there was one, of all the rest, whom she sighed to reach—to throw herself at his feet and confess her indebtedness and devote her life to his service." [4]

The climactic incident of the story is a coincidence which would certainly strain the credulity of the reader who expects the plot of a piece of fiction to follow the probable course of human events. Lily has a friend named Agnes Loyle who gives a party for the express purpose of bringing together her half brother and Lily herself. Her half brother is, of course, George Savage. The two confess their love for each other, the author disposes of the other characters in a final roundup, and the story concludes happily.

Judged by the standards of popular romance rather than those of belles lettres, Shillaber's romances are certainly successful. There is every indication that he was well acquainted with the stereotyped characters and the standard devices, style, and plots of the genre and that he was able to use them effectively to appeal to an audience attuned to the conventions of popular romance. He was also very adroit in manipulating characters and plots to stimulate in his readers the stock responses which they enjoyed. It is evident, however, from the strong suggestion of burlesque which runs throughout his romances, that Shillaber did not have the high regard for the romance as a literary form which he had for the anecdote, the localized sketch, and the comic tale. It is equally evident that he did not lavish the time and care on his romances that he did on his Partington pieces; and, as a result, they lack almost altogether the stylistic excellence and the depth of character portrayal which characterize the best of the Partington series.

II *Verse*

Like his romances, Shillaber's verse was written for a popular audience; most of it was published initially in the *Post*, the *Carpet Bag*, and the *Saturday Evening Gazette*. Except for what Shillaber himself included in *Rhymes With Reason and Without* and in *Lines in Pleasant Places*, his verse has not been collected; and, since it has little literary merit, it will no doubt remain uncollected. As a writer of verse, he possessed talent rather than genius, and he was not in the full sense of the word a poet. Shillaber, who was always modest about his ability as a writer of verse, states in his preface to *Rhymes With Reason and Without* that he wrote verse to amuse himself and his readers and that it is his hope that "their good nature may atone for lack of merit."[5]

As a writer of popular verse, Shillaber, as we would expect, used established verse forms and espoused traditional values. He employed the formal diction, the didacticism, the personifications, and the octosyllabic and heroic couplets which characterized the eighteenth-century verse which he had read as a schoolboy; but he also used themes, metrical patterns, and lyrical forms which were characteristic of contemporary verse. The value system reflected in this verse is that which was generally accepted by the middle class of the period. He treated simple themes like the dignity of work, the love of country, the tendency of wealth to corrupt, the positive moral influence of nature, the brotherhood of man, and the immortality of the soul in a manner which the average reader would both comprehend and agree with.

Strongly attracted to verse which was clear, direct, and rational, Shillaber rejected the abstract and philosophical poetry of the Transcendentalists: "The modern, hypercritical, transcendental idea of 'poetry' is too absurd to have a long life. It makes imagination, especially that of a dreamy, foggy character, of great account; while fancy, humor, wit, and sense go for little or nothing. With the admirers of this style of poetry it is the highest praise to be sublimely unintelligible or unintelligibly sublime. But a poetical theory which excludes half of Horace, two thirds of Pope, and the whole of Juvenal and Butler, as not entitled to the name of poetry is too preposterous to have much prevalence." [6]

Shillaber's lyric verse is much superior to his narrative verse, and his best lyrics are those in which he treats with genuine feeling the natural beauty of rural New England. Since many residents of Boston had, like Shillaber, migrated from the hinterland, his lyric responses to the seashore, the forests, the mountains, and the fields of the region no doubt had a strong appeal to his readers. Typical of this type of verse is "A Glance out into the Cool," a lyric which has as its theme the contrast between the coolness and tranquillity of the woods and the oppressive heat and activity of the city. Written in ballad stanzas, the poem expresses the writer's wish to escape from the hectic life of the city to the serenity of the forest:

> To where the pine-trees' mournful breathing
>   Lures the mind to peaceful themes,
> Like voices of some good spirit, wreathing
>   Heaven's sweet cadence with its dreams;
>
> To where, remote from habitation,
>   Within a deep and rocky dell,
> O'erarching trees, in exultation,
>   Guard in their shade the little well
>
> That through the rocky chancel stealeth,
>   With a low-murmuring song of bliss,
> Till brighter blooms the flower that feeleth
>   The inspiration of its kiss. [7]

Similar thematically to his nature lyrics are a number of verses which extol the humble life of the poor and simple people of rural New England. Characteristic of this group of verses is "The Cottage by the

Sea," a poem in which he idealizes the life of a fisherman who lives with his family in an isolated house on the seashore. The verses praise the simplicity and virtue of the fisherman who, because he lives and works close to elemental nature, has found a wisdom and happiness which are denied to men of wealth whose lives are divorced from nature:

> The tides that flow and the winds that blow,
>   And the sea-birds on the wing,
> And the clouds that rise in the changing skies,
>   To him all wisdom bring.
>
> . . . .
>
> Thus the fisherman lives most happy and free,
>   No other wealth doth crave
> Than the blessing of love and liberty,
>   And the product of the wave.[8]

In response no doubt to the current popularity of the ballad, Shillaber also wrote many mock or literary ballads in which he narrates stories taken from various sources. Since he possessed a considerable knowledge of the history and folklore of his native region, it is not surprising that in writing his ballads he should draw upon this fund of information. Typical of his ballads is "Ballad of the Piscataqua." Based on local history, the ballad narrates in a humorous vein a quarrel which arose between the New Hampshire cities of Dover and Portsmouth over the settlement of a piece of land called Bloody Fight Point. Although the conflict, which became a contest between Walter Neal and Thomas Wiggin, grew extremely heated, the dispute was settled peacefully and bloodshed was avoided:

> Then "Bloody Fight Point" that spot was hight;
>   Not from its hue, I ween,
> Nor yet for its ensanguined fight,
>   But for blood it *might* have seen,
>
> Had Captain Wiggin and Captain Neal
>   There met in mortal fight,
> And the arbitration of biting steel
>   Had settled their quarrel right.[9]

In another ballad entitled "The Witch of Lynn; or, a Good Many Years Ago" he narrates a story, perhaps drawn from New England folklore, of the defeat of a wicked witch by a young fisherman. The ballad tells how the hero, in spite of the dire threats of the Witch of Lynn, "launched his boat on the tide, / And dashed along through the spray." But the determined witch brews up a storm, and a large wave threatens to capsize the boat. When praying fails to stop the power of the witch, the hero wildly strikes the wave with his oar and the storm subsides. After the fisherman has finally struggled back to the shore, he finds that the witch has died under very mysterious circumstances:

> And cold and stiff her body he found,
>   And stranger than all the rest,
> It bore no sign of bruise or wound,
>   *Save an oar-blade mark on the breast.*[10]

In other verses Shillaber attempted, as John Greenleaf Whittier did in several of his poems, to preserve the memory of a vanishing way of life in New England; and, like Whittier, he was able to draw on an intimate personal knowledge of the texture of that life. Although these poems have little literary value, his nostalgic reminiscences of the life which he had known as a youth undoubtedly struck a responsive chord in many of his readers. In "The Quilting," he records his memory of the food, gossip, dancing, and singing which made the quilting bee a memorable social event in the lives of rural people.[11] "The Old Time Apple Bee" is a recollection in verse of the hard work and the simple pleasure which ensued when friends and neighbors gathered together to pick apples.[12] "Music of the Flail" describes the monotony and the muted cheerfulness of threshing on the barn floor during the cold winter months:

> Monotonous its tone; no mighty song
>   Is that which rises from the threshing-floor—
> Its time but measured by the heart-beats strong
>   Of him who long has conned its measure o'er;
> Its only listener, maybe, the sweet bird
>   That sits awaiting on the frozen spray,
> Or the slim weasel, that abroad has stirred,
>   Disturbed from its reflections in the hay.[13]

In "The Old Stage-Coach" he recalls the joy which he experienced as a boy when he was permitted to ride high upon the seat beside the driver of the coach and four. He concludes by expressing his regret that the romantic stagecoach has been superseded by the faster but much less exciting railway train.[14]

Another substantial group of Shillaber's verses were written to satisfy the contemporary popular taste for the moral and the didactic in verse. Hurriedly written and poor even by the standards of newspaper verse, these compositions, however, are not always endorsements of current popular values and attitudes. One of the most persistent themes of his didactic verse, for instance, is the condemnation of the widespread spirit of materialism and commercialism which was corrupting American life and endangering the ideals of American democracy. For example, in "Apples: An Analogy" he portrays a youthful apple seller who has already been infected by the virus of commercialism; as a result, he is crafty, cunning, dishonest, and speculative. He continues in a rather clumsy analogy to make the point that, like the boy, too many adults have become corrupted by their pursuit of money.[15]

In "A Sweet Revenge" he writes of a wealthy, powerful, and ruthless merchant who lived only for money; and, as a result, "Benevolence ne'er shone, / In one blest act, to mark his selfish way." But death, the great leveler, took him, just as it took the unfortunate people whom he refused to help, and those who knew him did not mourn his passing. The poor people whose plight he ignored have their revenge when they are rewarded by being admitted to heaven while the rich man is turned away:

> The beggars of earth who sought his aid,
> And turned unpitied from his door away,
> Stand in those heavenly courts in light arrayed,
> Where his weak vision may not dare to stray.[16]

Another vein which Shillaber frequently mined is the sentimental. The verse in this category, which is generally of inferior quality, commonly concerns the subject of death. Characteristic of this group is "The Consumptive," a poem which describes in a mawkish manner the final days of a woman dying of tuberculosis, a disease rampant at this time. After describing her pale cheeks and thin hands, the poem describes her patience as "She pressed her bed of pain . . " and waited for death to end her travail. The poem concludes with a typical nineteenth-century deathbed scene in which the victim's tearful friends and relatives gather around her and wait for the end.[17] Similar in tone is "On the Death of a Child," verses that treat a theme which, because of the high infant mortality rate, was very popular in the nineteenth century. In the verses the poet expresses his belief that, when the overwhelming grief is dissipated, reason will show "the dealing of a righteous God" and that eventually the grieving parents and the dead child will be reunited among the "immortal blest." [18]

Although his humorous verse lacks the excellence of his best humorous prose, it is superior to his didactic and sentimental verse. Generally narrative in form, his humorous poems often treat the eternally comic theme of love. "Parson Storer in a Fix; or, the Magic of a Kiss Misapplied," for example, is the humorous story in hexameters of an austere parson whose whole outlook on life is changed through an encounter with a serving girl. The parson, who is a caricature of the ascetic and narrow Protestant minister, is a bachelor who had always looked with some distaste and disfavor upon lovers and lovemaking. "But his breast experienced a flame that never there had glowed" after his servant girl mistook him one night for her secret lover and kissed him passionately on the mouth. Henceforth he was a kinder and gentler man.[19]

Written in a different vein, "The Song of the Jilted One" is a burlesque of the popular love poem. The rejected lover who is the narrator of the poem first describes the charms of his erstwhile love in the trite language of popular verse: "Her skin was fair,—oh! very fair,— / Her teeth were white as pearls." But he then proceeds to tell how she rejected him, married a seedy baker, had a dozen children, and became a tyrannical scold. The jilted lover concludes that he is now perfectly content to let the baker keep her and that he will not pine away like the typical rejected lover of the popular love poem.[20]

Mrs. Partington appears in a very limited number of Shillaber's verses, and none of those in which she appears is basically humorous. "Mrs. Partington at Tea," for instance, is a didactic rather than a humorous poem. As the poem begins, Mrs. Partington and Ike are sitting peacefully before the fire drinking tea; and, while his aunt gazes tenderly at the profile of her deceased husband which hangs on the wall, Ike spoils her cup of suchong tea by putting snuff in it. Shillaber concludes the poem with the following moral:

> This moral, you see,
> Is drawn from the tea
> That Isaac ruined for Mistress P.:

> Forever will mix in the cup of our joy
> The dark sappee of sorrow's alloy,
> And none are free,
> Any more than she,
> From annoying alloys that mix with their tea.[21]

"Mrs. Partington's Farewell When She Left the Post" expresses from the old dame's point of view the sincere regret which Shillaber felt in 1850 when he left the Boston *Post* to join the staff of the *Pathfinder and Railway Guide:*

> By the open door she stood,
> And a drop stood in her eye,—
> A thousand thronging memories
> Restrained the sad good-by;
> 'Twas sundering the golden chain
> That long had bound her here,
> And she gave to olden happiness
> The tribute of a tear.[22]

"Oracular Pearls Gathered from the Lips of Mrs. Partington" is simply an interesting collection of folk sayings in octosyllabic couplets. Although the sayings are put in the mouth of Mrs. Partington, the verses fail, partly at least because they are not in her language:

> If you laugh on a Monday in sportive delight,
> You will certainly cry before Saturday night.
> Tip over the salt, and the fat's in the fire,
> Forboding all trouble, dissension and ire.
> Twirl a whole apple-paring over your head
> 'Twil fall the initial of him you will wed.[23]

Without doubt, Shillaber experienced his greatest success as a writer of popular verse with his occasional pieces, many of which were written to be read at public gatherings. Composed to celebrate church, lodge, college, municipal, and state events as well as reunions, weddings, birthdays, and anniversaries, his occasional verse encompasses a wide range of themes, moods, and verse forms. His first occasional poems were published in the *Carpet Bag,* one of the earliest being "What Was It All About?" Written to celebrate in a humorous fashion the Great Railroad Jubilee which was held in Boston in 1851, the theme of the poem is that despite the fact that the president of the United States, the governor of Massachusetts, and many lesser dignitaries were in Boston to honor the event, the man in the street was blissfully unaware of what was going on:

> Well, the city of Boston "gin a treat,"
> And the people relished the noise and rout,
> Their voices were heard in every street,
> Hurraing loudly with lungs most stout;
> But we guess, of all who were there to see't,
> Very few knew what t' was all about.[24]

Shillaber, who loved his native state and enjoyed returning to it, wrote several occasional poems for reunions of natives of New Hampshire. In 1852, for instance, he wrote "New Hampshire," an invitation in verse to a gathering of the Sons of New Hampshire. The voice of the state calls, he writes, not for her sons to buckle on their swords and defend her soil but to attend the festivities and "For one brief hour to find release / From worldly strife and turmoil there."[25] He also wrote several poems to celebrate reunions of the Sons of Portsmouth, New Hampshire.

Cast in octosyllabic couplets, "Home Again" was written to be delivered at a reunion in Portsmouth on July 4, 1853. In these verses he reminisces nostalgically about Breakfast Hill, Puddle Dock, Waller's Mill, and other landmarks which he loved as a child.[26] This was the first time that he had read a poem in public, and he records in "Experiences During Many Years" that, although he was very apprehensive, his courage revived when he began to read and his presentation was successful.[27] Again on July 4, 1873, he read original verses entitled "Twenty Years Later" at another reunion of the Sons of Portsmouth. After telling how natives of Portsmouth are scattered over the world and describing the changes which have occurred in the city since they left it, he concludes sentimentally with the statement that, although his verses may not be eloquent, they are true to the thought "That brings us, children, home again, / Beside our mother's knee to stand."[28]

One of the proudest moments of Shillaber's life was the occasion on which he read an original poem before the literary societies of Dartmouth College at the commencement exercises in July, 1871. He later recorded that he accepted the invitation in January with considerable hesitation, worked very hard on the composition, and felt more and more inadequate to the task as the day approached. Entitled

"The Mound Builders," the verses which he read at the exercises were very well received, and he was much flattered by the enthusiastic response to his effort. Written in heroic couplets, the long poem is constructed around an analogy between the efforts of the prehistoric Indian tribes in Illinois to construct their huge burial mounds and modern man's efforts to make something memorable of his life. Directing his verse at the graduates, he asks them to build their mounds with honesty, integrity, and devotion so that, "When angels, searching for its inner plan, / Shall say, approvingly, HERE WAS A MAN! " [29]

Shillaber, a gregarious man, was a "joiner" who belonged to several fraternal organizations and who, because of his facility in writing occasional verse, was invited to read original verse to honor special occasions at lodges throughout New England. Typical of these is "Twenty-One," verses which were written to celebrate the twenty-first anniversary of the Star of Bethlehem Lodge of Chelsea, Massachusetts. Written in octosyllabic couplets, the poem turns on the analogy of a man's having reached maturity and the lodge's having reached the same age and condition. The central theme of the poem is that, just as age alone does not make a man virtuous, neither does it make an organization worthwhile:

> And time alone, don't make the man;
> For eighty years were but a span
> If spent in simply selfish aims,
> Regardless of another's claims.

The true purpose of a fraternal organization, the poem concludes, is the unselfish one of helping others in times of sorrow and need.[30]

Intensely loyal to the craft of printing and an active member of the Boston Typographical Society, Shillaber also wrote numerous verses to celebrate printers and printing. On October 6, 1856, for example, he read original verses in Portsmouth at the Centennial Anniversary of the Establishment of the Press in New Hampshire. Entitled "A Hundred Years Ago," the poem, after recounting in some detail the history of Portsmouth, tells of the founding of the New Hampshire *Gazette,* the first newspaper in the state.[31] Years later Shillaber remembered with amusement that, when he had finished reading the verses, a distinguished listener patted him on the back and earnestly said, "You done well." [32]

On January 19, 1874, he read an original poem entitled "Press and

Press People" at the fiftieth anniversary of the founding of the Franklin Typographical Society of Boston. The poem opens with lines which pay tribute to the craft of printing for the educational opportunities which it offers those who follow it:

> We prize our venerable Art,
> Our fondly cherished Alma Mater;
> With discipline she tried our heart,
> And taught us thus to venerate her.

The poet then points to the importance of the press in a free society and to the considerable debt which people in other walks of life owe to the people of the press. It concludes with lines praising the benevolence of the members of the Franklin Typographical Society and congratulating the organization on its fiftieth anniversary.[33]

Another category of Shillaber's occasional verse is constituted of lines written to mark important events in the lives of people whom he admired. "Welcome to Jenny Lind," for example, was written to greet the famous Swedish singer when she arrived in Boston during her first tour of America in 1850.[34] "Congratulatory" was written to felicitate his old acquaintance Mark Twain on his marriage to Olivia Langdon on February 2, 1870, and to compliment him upon the reputation he had achieved as a writer.[35] Other poems in this group were written to commemorate the deaths of personal friends and public figures. "Daniel Webster Is No More," for instance, was composed on the occasion of the death of the great statesman on October 24, 1852. Although Webster was a Whig and Shillaber a Democrat, he paid him tribute in solemn verses which undoubtedly reflected the mood of the nation when the great statesman died:

> 'Twas Sabbath morning, still and clear,
> And fair uprose the ruddy sun,
> When burst upon our startled ear
> The booming of the mournful gun.
>
> The sound of fear smote every breast,
> As echoing round from hill to shore,
> It broke the peaceful Sabbath-rest,
> Proclaiming Webster was no more! [36]

"Miles O'Reilly," one of Shillaber's most poignant and heartfelt poems, was written on the death of Charles Graham Halpine, a writer who had been one of his partners in the founding of the *Carpet Bag* and who had produced a number of humorous pieces for that magazine under the pseudonym "Miles O'Reilly." After praising Halpine for his "fierce ambition, recklessness, and pride" and for his performance as an officer in the Civil War, Shillaber lauds him for his ability as a satirist:

> His was the caustic pen that ever sought
> To prick the bubble of a vain pretence;
> He strove by song, with wit and satire fraught,
> To banish wrong and bold incompetence.[37]

One final group of Shillaber's poems which merit some attention is that comprised of his Civil War lyrics. Most of his war verses appeared initially in the *Gazette,* and the best of them were later collected by Shillaber in *Lines in Pleasant Places* under the heading "War Lyrics."[38] "Massachusetts," the first poem in the group, expresses with genuine feeling the upsurge of Union sentiment which followed the attack on Fort Sumter as well as Shillaber's pride in the fact that Massachusetts was the first state to answer President Lincoln's call on April 15, 1861, for seventy-five thousand volunteers. "The Sixth at Baltimore," the second poem in the section, commemorates the occasion when the first blood was spilled in the war. The poem relates how the Sixth Massachusetts Regiment, the first militia regiment to answer Lincoln's call, was attacked by private citizens of Baltimore on April 19, the eighty-sixth anniversary of the Battle of Lexington and Concord, while it was on its way to Washington. It concludes by expressing the hope that the death of the militiamen killed in the attack will strengthen the resolution of the North:

> The dead return, the arms to nerve
> And strengthen hearts that else might swerve;
> They speak again, from the silent sod,
> In a voice that stirs like the voice of God,
> And heroes vow, from their hearts' deep core,
> To follow the Sixth through Baltimore.

"The Way We Went to Beaufort" celebrates the success of the Port Royal expedition, a major piece of Union strategy designed to provide a base in Port Royal Harbor, South Carolina, for blockading the Southern coast. The success of this expedition, which was carried out late in

1861, was the first major Union victory of the war; and it heartened immensely the discouraged supporters of the Union cause:

> A thrill pervaded the loyal land
> When the gladdening tidings came to hand;
> Each heart felt joy's emotion;
> The cloud of gloom and doubt dispersed,
> The sun of hope through the darkness burst,
> And the zeal the patriot's heart had nurst
> Burned with a warm devotion.

"Grierson's Raid" was written to commemorate the successful conclusion of a cavalry raid led by Colonel B. H. Grierson in April and May, 1863. The raid, part of U. S. Grant's Vicksburg campaign, was one of the most daring and effective of the entire war; it pursued a scorched-earth policy by burning bridges, wrecking rail lines, and disrupting communications over a wide area between La Grange, Tennessee, and Baton Rouge, Louisiana. It was, as the verses indicate, a frightening experience for the Confederacy:

> 'Twas a brave bold dash through the hostile land
> That scattered terror on every hand,
> Making the rebel heart afraid
> At the daring valor of Grierson's Raid!

"Poor Boy" is a typically sentimental poem about the grief of a mother who has lost her son in the war. "War Changes," which is written from the point of view of a "peace" Democrat, tells how a pacifist is caught up in spite of himself in the hysteria engendered by the war. "The Old War Ship," the final poem in the section, was almost certainly written to mark the occasion when the frigate *Constitution,* or "Old Ironsides" as Oliver Wendell Holmes had called her years earlier, was towed during the first months of the war from Annapolis to Newport, Rhode Island. The old ship was moved when the United States Naval Academy was transferred to Newport as a precaution against its being captured by the Confederacy.

Rather than writing for posterity, Shillaber in his verse attempted to please a wide contemporary audience; and, as a result, it can be fairly evaluated only within the context of the popular culture of nineteenth-century America. Judging from the large volume of verse which he published over a long period of time, it is evident that he gauged accurately the values and tastes of his readers. But because popular values and tastes changed toward the end of the century, succeeding generations have found little of interest in Shillaber's verse; consequently, it has been completely forgotten except by a few students of the popular culture of the era.

CHAPTER 6

Lectures in Verse

INAUGURATED in 1826 in Millbury, Massachusetts, the lyceum movement reached the height of its popularity in the 1830's when about three thousand lyceums were organized in at least fifteen states between the Atlantic Ocean and the Mississippi River. Designed as a system of popular education to meet the demands of the middle and lower classes for information and moral inspiration, lyceums served as an important shaping force on American literature, education, and popular culture for several decades. Louis Agassiz, Horace Mann, James Russell Lowell, Ralph Waldo Emerson, Henry Ward Beecher, Charles Sumner, and a host of lesser luminaries traveled about the country during the lecture season popularizing knowledge and moral values. Starved for culture and eager for self-improvement, the American people gladly paid their money to hear lectures on natural science, history, literature, religion, philosophy, politics, travel, and other subjects.

By 1855, the year in which Shillaber first attempted lecturing, the lyceum as an educational institution had degenerated, and audiences were demanding lectures of a more entertaining and superficial nature. Lectures were being sponsored by library societies and young men's associations rather than by lyceum committees; and, although wholly humorous lectures were not yet acceptable, audiences expected lecturers to "sell" them by combining liberal amounts of entertainment with information and moral instruction. In response to contemporary public taste, Shillaber attempted to meet the expectations of his audiences with a mixture of humor, sentimentality, inspiration, and moralizing.

I *The Lecturer*

Since Shillaber had achieved national popularity as the creator of Mrs. Partington before he entered the field of lecturing, he could depend upon his reputation as a humorous writer to attract listeners to his lectures. But the popular reputation which he had achieved as creator of Mrs. Partington was also a handicap because his audiences expected him to impersonate his literary creation on the lecture platform, and he steadfastly refused to do so: "Mrs. Partington was the one wanted, but I would not make a mountebank of myself. Artemus Ward wrote me from Cleveland, 'Come out here, as the old woman, put on the cap and specs, and you will carry the town.' Josh Billings wrote me, 'Trot out the old dame.' But I would not, to my cost, and sacrificed a fortune for a sentiment." [1] Since many people in his audiences had come with the expectation of seeing Mrs. Partington on the platform, Shillaber usually prefaced his lecures by apologizing for not bringing his double to speak for him. [2]

Shillaber's presentations were not really "lectures" in the usual sense of the word; instead, they were recitations or readings of rhymed doggerel in the genteel tradition. Even though he had achieved popularity as a reader of original occasional verse before he attempted lecturing, he seemingly obtained the idea of the rhymed lecture from other lecturers rather than from his own experience as an occasional poet. The example of Oliver Wendell Holmes, who in his Lowell Institute Lectures on the subject of "English Poets of the Nineteenth Century" in 1853 began the custom of concluding his discourses with original verse, may have encouraged Shillaber to attempt complete lectures in verse. [3] It is more likely, however, that it was John G. Saxe and Park Benjamin, both of whom delivered humorous and satirical lectures in verse early in the decade of the 1850's, who furnished the inspiration as well as the models for Shillaber's lectures. [4]

Although the rhymed lectures of Saxe, Benjamin, and Shillaber were neither highly artistic nor extremely successful, they are important historically because they serve as a link between the serious lyceum lecture and the pure entertainment of Artemus Ward, the first really successful literary comedian in America. Probably because of current sentiment against the wholly comic lecture, Shillaber himself emphasized the moral and inspirational qualities rather than the humor of his lectures. In a letter to H. H. Bigelow he wrote, "But do not lay too much stress on the fun of my productions—I have only studied to make them pleasant. My aim has been to make people feel better, rather than funny." [5]

A newspaper reporter said of his lecture "Life's Bright Side," "It was not so funny as many had anticipated—its humor not displaying in any sudden flashes or epigrammatic clap traps, but was mildly diffused and made accessory rather than principal in the performance." [6] Although few reviewers commented on Shillaber's delivery, he seems to have relied for effect upon his material rather than upon his presentation of it. Unlike Artemus Ward and Mark Twain, he did not attempt to play the role of literary comedian on the lecture platform; and he apparently was not the commanding presence on the platform that Twain and Ward were.

If Shillaber was not an overwhelming success as a lecturer, neither was he an utter failure; and he seems to have experienced no difficulty in scheduling engagements to speak. During the season of 1857–58, he traveled as far west as the Mississippi River, lecturing in Cleveland, Chicago, Cincinnati, Evansville, Clarksville (Tennessee), and in other cities of the South and Middle West.[7] In "Experiences During Many Years" he records that for two winters, probably those of 1857–58 and 1858–59, he was almost constantly on the trains, and he estimates that, while on his lecture tours, he slept in more than two hundred towns.[8] Reactions to his lectures by newspaper reporters, as one would expect, were varied and contradictory. A reporter in Clarksville, Tennessee, praised him for his "happy elocution," "genial humor," "pungent wit," and "genial philosophy"; [9] but a reporter in Cincinnati wrote, "Mr. S's 'Bright Side of Life' was, as we have said, in rhyme, though hardly in rhythm, but very far removed from poetry. There are occasional good couplets, but the greater portion reminded us very much of the carriers' addresses of country newspapers, which in our journalistic experience, it has been our misfortune to meet." [10]

II *The Lectures*

Shillaber apparently had several lectures in his repertory. In the letter to H. H. Bigelow mentioned above he writes that he has prepared rhymed lectures entitled "Men and Women," "The Street, " and "The Press" and that he is presently composing one on the subject of "Household Words." [11] Evidence that he actually delivered "Men and Women" or "Household Words" has not been uncovered, but he did undoubtedly present the other two from the platform. In the winter of 1855 he made his debut as a lecturer with "The Press" when he presented it first in Boston and then in nearby towns and cities.[12] "The Street" he seems to have used for second-night stands on his lecture tours of 1857–58.[13] Melville D. Landon in *Kings of the Platform and Pulpit* includes a composition in prose entitled "The Partington

Lecture," which consists of a number of previously published Mrs. Partington anecdotes strung together with no thematic unity. Although the annotations in the text of the composition suggest that it was delivered as a lecture, no external evidence has been discovered to prove that it actually was presented from the platform.[14]

Shillaber's mainstay on his tours of 1857—58 and 1858—59 was a long composition in rhymed doggerel variously entitled "The Bright Side of Life," "Life's Bright Side," and "The Life of Man." This lecture, which was advertised as "A Rhymed Exercise of a serio-comic character," was basically an amplification of Shakespeare's seven stages of man.[15] According to a reporter in the Evansville (Indiana) *Daily Journal,* the rather thin, platitudinous thematic content of the lecture was as follows:

From it all, he deduced the moral that all we term *living* is not life—that it is not living, merely to consume years by an inglorious and selfish inactivity and self-indulgence, but that it must be measured by the uses to which it is put. By this standard of measurement, he said, a life of four score selfishly spent might be regarded as a span, not to be compared in worth to the brief existence of a child whose life was full of love. . . . From this he reasoned that we should be bigger, and truer hearted, and admit our brother's claim in God's heritage to be as good as our own, and that we should not, too readily, in our fancied superiority, condemn unfortunate man, not knowing how much of temptation he had resisted, while resistance, though seemingly fruitless, might count as success with Him who can read the heart.[16]

"Life's Bright Side" was never published, and the manuscript has not come to light; but the lecture was extensively reported in a number of newspapers. The following account from the Cincinnati *Gazette,* December 7, 1857, provides an excellent summary of the lecture:

LADIES AND GENTLEMEN:—Before I commence what I have prepared for your pleasure, allow me to say a word for myself. I am by reputation placed in the rank of funny men, but I beg to assure the universe that of all my witticisms there was no malice aforethought in their conception. I had points to make and the sugar coating was necessary to make them go down. It never entered my heart to conceive the idea of being funny on the rostrum. The effort would be as painful to me as that of the enterprising young butcher who set up on his own hook. (Applause)

Sampson was once called to make sport for a large and appreciative audience, (as the newspapers no doubt termed it) and he brought down the house; (applause) but that was positively his last appearance on any stage, (applause) and I am afraid that would be my fate if I should try it.

He then announced the subject of his lecture as "Life's Bright Side," and said, "I do not believe in the everlasting practice of picking man to pieces to show his bad points. I use the generic name man, though I intend also to embrace the woman (applause) in the scope of my applications."

> How much men know! they scale the highest stars,
> Compute in inches all the way to Mars—
> Measure the belt round Jupiter's broad waist,
> And tell how bright Saturn's rings are placed;
> Decide how fast the light would have to run
> To get to earth when started from the sun;
> Point out on starry plains the nebulae pale,
> And point the moral of a comet's tail. (Applause)

"Dear me, how fluidly he does talk! " exclaimed Mrs. Partington; "I am always rejoined when he mounts the nostrum, for his eloquence warms me in every nerve and cartridge of my body. Verdigris itself couldn't be more smooth than his blessed tongue is."

The audience evidently supposed the first rhyming lines a quotation, and patiently waited for the lecture, but the funny man went on rhyming in that measure all the way through.

We give below the following specimens.
Of youth he said:

> Guardian angels hedge around his glee,
> And keep life's acrid pickles from his tea.

> * * * * * * * * *

> I would not see the trace of anxious years
> On faces where the bloom of youth appears;
> I would not have the radiant, joyous eye
> Cobweb'd by premature antiquity;
> With ledgers indexed in its every beam,
> And latent speculation in its gleam;
> Even to win what many youth have done,
> The hundreds banked at early twenty-one.

He alluded to the natural instincts of youth and how true they were
to those instincts although there were exceptions to the rule.

Where youth before 'tis scarce from childhood freed,
Becomes a fossil or has gone to seed;
Like some precocious sapling of a pear,
That though a young ambition learns to bear.

He then spoke of the mingling of the sexes in youth, and proceeded
to show that, only through such mingling, could the purity of both be
preserved, he'd have more hope of a rising son of his if under female
influence he but chose to shine.

Than if he shed in solitude his ray,
Or cut up shines in any other way;
Red lips as nice as strawberries and cream,
Delude him on through many a wildering dream,
Youth rhymes unmeasured in its dear one's praise
And like a pullet perpetrates its lays.

He regarded the rhyme as a sort of Russia salve to heal the
heart—professing to have tried it himself, and tested its efficacy, but
cautioned youth to beware of ink, but write their words in paregoric or
onion juice, that was soothing and tearful, exactly fitting to the case
should not militate against the individual.

When the change comes, and early sentiment
Has found some later reasons to repent

He proceeded to describe the life of man—giving illustrations of its
importance—best seen

——In love's ennobling aims
Proving the lesson which should not be lost
That he is happiest who loves the most

He cautioned people against selling their souls for money, like "Tom
Walker" in the storybook, presenting it as

A warning that at every bosom knocks
Disposed to dabble in such fancy stocks.

MANHOOD

But grand the manhood wealth can never buy
That looks the tempting Syren in the eye,
Listing the pleasant clink of ready tin,
But heeding the most the monitor within.

❋   ❋   ❋   ❋   ❋   ❋   ❋   ❋   ❋   ❋

Wealth in such hands becomes a blessed means
To scatter light over many darkened scenes.

         *   *   *   *   *   *   *   *

His soul has sunshine in its very glance
And in his deeds his prayers have audience
Who says God bless you, and who means it too,
And in love's grammar acts the verb to do.

THE TRADESMAN

The tradesman leads an ever watchful dance,
To take advantage of the lucky chance.
Alas! the lucky chance was dimly shown
Where bankruptcy of late upreared its throne;
And care's rude touch o'erwhelmed the anxious heart,
And *dolours* more than dollars crowned the mart.
A lesson teaching us that we must learn
To gauge our needs by the amount we earn—
To shun extravagance—that fearful evil—
As sedulously as we would the d—deceiver of souls
From fashion's thraldom all our skirts to free,
And re-unite a wise economy.

THE DOCTOR

Feels our pulses and our tongues explore,
Then guess the causes we have guessed before;
And write in mystic scrawl, with R prefixed,
For aqua pura and sach alva, mixed;
Or *hydrar*-something, *hydra* nearest right,
Not heavens *mercury* by a mighty sight.

MARRIAGE

Marriage is man's inevitable state,
To which by nature he must emigrate
If to himself he's true; or else unblest,
His life were only 'alf and 'alf at best.
Woman and man are one by nature's plan,
And man unmarried is but half a man.

THE FIRST BABY

Do you remember when those little eyes
First flashed upon your own with glad surprise,
How proud you felt and how with step elate
You walked the pave with more than regal gait?

*   *   *   *   .   *   *   *

There's not a moment in a mortal's life
So full of pride, with ecstasy so rife,
As when he holds in all its budding charms,
His first born baby in his manly arms.

THE BABY'S DEAD

And blest the home where grief's afflictive hand
Press on the heart strings of the little band,
When from its midst the fairest one has fled,
And hopes that round it clung are chill and dead.

*   *   *   *   *   *   *   *   *

'Tis through the shades of bitter woe and pain,
That we alone a fruitage high attain,
The darkest wave that lifts us by its might,
Brings us the nearest to the heavenly light.

He berates woman as the cause of Adam's fall.

And but for thee we might today be found
In Eden's blest and consecrated ground,
Unplagued by thought of business or of care,
Content e'en though we nothing had to wear.

A WIFE

Much as we prize the highest good in life,
We would not wish an angel for a wife;
But be content with what is far more common,
A genial hearted, true and loving woman.

OLD AGE

How grand is age, when virtue's gentle ray
Imparts his warmth to life's declining day,
And in the cheerfulness of its control,
Instals the Indian summer of the soul.
Here the secret of respect doth dwell:
To be respected, be respectable.

MRS. PARTINGTON

How *sage* her counsels! like a bowl of tea
From sage decocted, and a melody,
Like some old harpsichord, endows her tongue,
Which drops its sweets the listening crowds among.

SPIRITS

Not all of living is what we call life,
To feel its fever 'mid its cares and strife,
To fret away its hours in useless groans,
And vex the marrow of the spirit's bones.
I make no bones at using such a figure,
Since spirits now are full of vim and vigor.

CHILD'S PARENTHESIS

More than a life to reckon time by bliss
Is spann'd by arms in fond parenthesis,
Where like a flowery garland they bedeck
Childhood's sweet altar—the maternal neck.

THE LESSON OF LIFE

And heeding it and laying it to heart,
We'd more successfully enact our part,
And oftener in Life's perplexing school
We'd make the square on universal rule.

CONCLUSION

Kind friends who've followed me with patient ear
I close my story, wearisome I fear;
Yet here and there amidst the leaves and grass,
A flower or two you may have chanced to pass,
And if remembered, place them in your breast,
That best herbarium 'neath your spacious vest.[17]

If "Life's Bright Side" was typical of Shillaber's lectures, it is evident that he planned them primarily as popular entertainment and that both the form and content of his productions were designed to make as many appeals as possible to contemporary public taste. The doggerel verse in which the lecture is cast not only was calculated to amuse with puns, slang, and witticisms but was also intended to satisfy the popular appetite for sentimentality. He also attempted to meet the desire of his audience for moral instruction; but, instead of questioning the conventional moral code as Emerson and Thoreau did in their lectures, he simply affirmed the traditional middle-class values which his listeners already accepted. He endorsed marriage and parenthood; and he asserted his belief in honesty, love, conscientiousness, benevolence, prudence, cheerfulness, philanthropy, and respectability. Conversely, he warned his listeners against cupidity, extravagance, selfishness, and financial speculation. Clearly conceived to amuse and to reinforce traditional morality, the lecture has no literary value, but it is important historically as a link between the serious lyceum and the comic lecture, and it is an interesting piece of Americana.

CHAPTER 7

Reputation and Achievement

DESPITE the national popularity which Shillaber enjoyed during the years when he was publishing the Mrs. Partington sketches and the prestige which he attained as a newspaper and magazine editor, he was nearly forgotten by the older generation and was almost completely unknown to younger readers when he died in 1892 at the age of seventy-eight. There has been no revival of interest in him or in his work since his death, and today he is known only to specialists in American humor. His books have been out of print for many years, he is seldom included in popular anthologies of American humor, and he receives little or no attention in standard histories of American literature. Furthermore, no extended scholarly study of him has thus far been published. Indeed, were it not for the limited but valuable pioneering work of Walter Blair and Franklin J. Meine, very few students of American literature would know that Shillaber had ever existed.

I Reputation

Like most other humorists of the nineteenth century, Shillaber received a minimum of serious attention from contemporary literary critics and scholars. Nineteenth-century literary study was focused almost exclusively on writers working in the genteel tradition, and native American humor had not yet gained respectability. Shillaber's excellence as a humorist was recognized early in his career, however, by two prominent members of the literary Establishment. Oliver Wendell Holmes in one of his lectures in the series entitled "English Poets of the Nineteenth Century," delivered in New York in December, 1853, said in discussing Thomas Hood, the British humorist, that "Humor is infinitely rarer than wit. I think there has been little of it since Burns. Humor must have feeling in it; wit needs none. Voltaire was a wit, but

Mrs. Partington's conversation with the omnibus driver has more feeling and humor than all he ever uttered. As laughter and weeping are closely allied, so pathos and humor are akin." [1]
Henry Ward Beecher, writing in the New York *Independent* at about the same time, also lauded Shillaber's humor:

Here we have opened another and most genuinely American vein of humor. Mr. Shillaber has certainly developed a peculiar phase of wit. The innocent verbal blunders of the most worthy Mrs. Partington are secondary to the sly humor often conveyed in the mistakes. There is a great deal of fragmentary picture drawing in the accompaniments, which, if performed upon canvass, would have given Mr. Shillaber rank with the best Dutch and Flemish artists. Sam Slick has run his race. Mrs. Partington is now the American humorist; original, genial, laughable, and not uninstructive. [2]

The first two published collections of Shillaber's humor received good reviews in the better magazines. In a review of *The Life and Sayings of Mrs. Partington* in *Harper's Magazine,* for example, the anonymous writer acknowledged "The unexampled popularity attained by these specimens of native humor" and praised Shillaber for his skill in characterization and his mastery of colloquial style:

The character of the oracular old dame is sustained with dramatic harmony throughout the whole of her unique comments; she never by any mischance relapses into orthodox English; and always hides beneath her eccentricity of expression the largest and warmest soul of grandmotherly kindness. Her biographer and "honest chronicler" has succeeded to a charm in giving the veracious history of her life. His irrepressible love of fun is so blended with the true spirit of wit, as to entitle him to a high rank in the walk to which he has so cordially devoted himself. He is certainly a master in this line—at the very top of the scale—and his imitators are—nowhere. [3]

After the publication in 1854 of *Life and Sayings of Mrs. Partington,* Shillaber was considered prominent enough as a writer by George W. Bungay to be included in his *Off-Hand Takings; or Crayon Sketches of the Noticeable Men of Our Age.* Bungay wrote, "Mr. Shillaber has, within a few years, won a reputation which some lovers of notoriety would give a dukedom to possess. His strange speeches have been copied in all portions of our country; they have crossed the sea and kindled smiles on faces in foreign lands."[4] Subsequent collections of Shillaber's humor did not receive so much attention by critics, and they were less enthusiastically received by the reading public.

Although most of Shillaber's books were out of print by the time he died and he was nearly forgotten, his death did not go unnoticed. *Harper's Weekly* carried a generous account of his life and achievement;[5] and the *New England Magazine* published a lengthy panegyric by Elizabeth Akers Allan.[6] In 1917, Will D. Howe, writing in *The Cambridge History of American Literature,* devoted a paragraph to Shillaber in which he made the observation that Mrs. Partington and Ike are "striking prototypes" of Mark Twain's Aunt Polly and Tom Sawyer.[7] He was merely mentioned, however, in 1925 in Jennette Tandy's *Crackerbox Philosophers in American Humor and Satire,* the first full-length scholarly study of the homespun tradition in American humor.[8] In 1933 in one of a series of articles on American comic periodicals, Franklin J. Meine discussed the *Carpet Bag* and stressed its importance as a liaison between the first and second generations of native humorists.[9]

It was not until 1937, however, that Walter Blair presented in *Native American Humor (1800–1900)* the first scholarly estimate of Shillaber's contribution to American humor. In this study Blair placed him squarely in the mainstream of our native comic tradition and rated him as one of the principal figures in the Down East school of humor.[10] In 1942 Blair included an excellent analysis of Shillaber's humor in *Horse Sense in American Humor.*[11] Since that time, no scholarly work of any consequence on Shillaber has been published.

II   *Achievement*

Despite the neglect which Shillaber has suffered at the hands of critics and scholars, he remains a foremost representative of our native humor. Although his humor, like that of most other nineteenth-century humorists, is fragmentary and incomplete, the quality of his writing is nevertheless high; and he created a gallery of memorable and varied characters against a convincing local background. Mrs. Partington is as convincingly and consistently drawn as Jack Downing, Sam Slick, or Birdofredum Sawin; and Ike Partington represents one of the first successful attempts in American literature to create a real boy. The excellence of his portraits of Mrs. Partington and Ike undoubtedly helped to overcome contemporary contempt for rustic and illiterate characters.

Shillaber also added a new dimension to Yankee humor when he portrayed his rustic characters against the background of a real urban center rather than an imaginary country village, dramatizing the startling incongruities between American urban and rural life and character. The style of the Partington pieces is important, too, since it was a notable contribution to a movement toward a new American prose style—one based on vernacular speech.

Shillaber's creation of Blifkins was also a significant achievement; for Blifkins is clearly a prototype of the Little Man, the dominant character type of twentieth-century humor. Other characters of this kind may have been created during the nineteenth century; but, if they were, they have not been recovered by modern scholars. Although Shillaber's background was rural, he lived most of his life in Boston and was well aware of the tensions and frustrations which beset city dwellers. As a result, Blifkins is convincingly drawn and is a much more modern character than Mrs. Partington.

Shillaber is also important because of the part which he played in the general onslaught on the sentimentality and overrefinement of the genteel tradition, an onslaught which was a basic element in the nineteenth-century comic tradition. Although his attitude toward the genteel was ambiguous and although he did write quantities of stereotyped genteel verse and fiction, it is nevertheless true that his best writing and the writing he took most seriously followed the vernacular rather than the genteel tradition. His Partington sketches, filled with gibes at the institutions and values of genteel culture, provided an antidote to it. Ike Partington was designed as a foil to the priggish heroes of the genteel books for boys, and the values embraced in his books for boys are in opposition to those of the established culture. Wideswarth was created as a satiric device to expose the absurdity of decadent Romantic idealism, one facet of genteel culture. It is true that Shillaber made no significant contribution to a new and vigorous Realistic fiction, but he and his fellow humorists helped to lay the groundwork for a new fiction both by their continual attacks on the genteel and by firmly grounding their own work in American character and life.

Although Shillaber was not a militant social critic, his social satire is not insignificant. His attacks on the reform movement, religious cults, Victorian moral standards, and slavery were vigorous and effective. A firm Jacksonian Democrat, he vigorously, and sometimes angrily, assailed those who would subvert the democratic ideals of freedom, equality, and justice. Aware of the defects of human nature and the dangers of unlimited democracy, he was nevertheless confident that people could and should govern themselves. Because most of his satire deals with matters which are now dead issues, however, it is of interest today only to the historian.

Shillaber was an influence on other writers both through the example of his own humor and through his position as editor of the *Carpet Bag.* The influence of his own humor is impossible to assess with any degree of accuracy or assurance. Younger humorists like Charles Farrar Browne, Henry Wheeler Shaw, and Marietta Holley certainly owed a considerable debt to the Down East school of humor since all of them used rustic characters, colloquial language, and the monologue. But whether the example of Shillaber specifically helped to shape their work is problematical.

His probable influence on Twain's *The Adventures of Tom Sawyer* has been pointed out by Walter Blair.[12] As Blair rightly asserts, the resemblance of Aunt Polly and Tom Sawyer to Mrs. Partington and Ike is remarkable; and Shillaber's characters are certainly prototypes of Twain's, whether or not Twain was directly influenced by Shillaber. Like Mrs. Partington, Aunt Polly is a tenderhearted widow who is rearing an orphaned nephew; and like Ike, Tom is a mischievous boy who misbehaves in church, plays hookey from school, teases cats, and tricks his aunt. He also plays pirate; and, like Ike, he uses as his source of inspiration Judson's *The Black Avenger of the Spanish Main.* The close resemblance between Aunt Polly and Mrs. Partington is strikingly evidenced by the fact that the frontispiece for *Life and Sayings of Mrs. Partington,* which is labeled "Ruth Partington," appeared in *The Adventures of Tom Sawyer* in 1876 under the label "Contentment," undoubtedly representing Aunt Polly.

Shillaber's most direct influence on American humor was exerted through his editing of the *Carpet Bag.* Despite the short life of the magazine, it was a potent force in determining the course of American humor for nearly half a century. It not only stimulated and published the younger generation of humorists but also provided an opportunity for them to learn the craft of writing under the tutelage of established humorists like Shillaber, Halpine, and Trowbridge. Although the magazine's chief claim to fame is the fact that it published the first known work of George Horatio Derby ("The New Uniform," April 3 and May 1, 1852); of Charles Farrar Browne ("An Incident," December 27, 1851); and of Samuel Langhorne Clemens ("The Dandy Frightening the Squatter," May 1, 1852), it should also be remembered that one hundred-odd lesser-known humorists from all over the country also contributed to it and were encouraged by it. Shillaber himself believed that it stimulated the writing of humor and helped to establish the humorous column as a standard feature of American newspapers.[13]

Benjamin Penhallow Shillaber was an accomplished journalist, a competent editor, and a gifted humorist. A devotee of reason, he maintained his sanity and sense of humor during a tumultuous and trying period in American history. Although he lacked the breadth of vision and the creative force of Twain, he was talented; and his total achievement is a significant one. He does not merit a place in the front ranks of American writers, but neither does he deserve to be completely forgotten.

Notes and References

Chapter One

1. For a discussion of the Down East school of humor see Walter Blair, *Native American Humor (1800–1900)* (New York, 1937), pp. 38–62.

2. The only detailed source of information about Shillaber is his "Experiences During Many Years," *New England Magazine,* VIII (1893), 511–25, 618–27, 719–24; IX (1893), 88–95, 153–60, 529–33, 625–31; X (1894), 29–36, 247–56, 286-94. The most complete sketch of his ancestry and early life is found in a letter in the Chicago Historical Society Library from Shillaber to an unknown recipient, February 21, 1879. Also helpful is the one published book about Shillaber: Cyril Clemens, *Shillaber* (Webster Groves, Missouri, 1946).

3. Undated letter from Shillaber to unknown correspondent (Chicago Historical Society Library).

4. *Lines in Pleasant Places* (Chelsea, Massachusetts, 1874), p. 30. Hereafter referred to as *Lines.*

5. "After-Dinner Effort," *Lines,* p. 129.

6. Arthur M. Schlesinger, Jr., *The Age of Jackson* (Boston, 1946), pp. 146–47.

7. Boston *Post,* September 28, 1854.

8. *Ibid.,* November 1, 1848.

9. George W. Bungay, *Off-Hand Takings; or Crayon Sketches of the Noticeable Men or Our Age* (New York, 1854), p. 376.

10. Boston *Post,* November 3, 1847, and December 14, 1847.

11. *Ibid.,* June 10, 1846.

12. *Ibid.,* May 27, 1847.

13. *Ibid.,* June 29, 1847.

14. Sydney Smith, "Mrs. Partington in Politics," *The World's Best Orations,* ed. David J. Brewer *et al.,* IX (St. Louis, 1900), 3479–81.

15. Information on the *Carpet Bag* can be found in the following two references: Frank Luther Mott, *A History of American Magazines,* II

130

(Cambridge, Massachusetts, 1938), 180—81; Franklin J. Meine, "The Carpet Bag," *The Collectors' Journal,* IV (October—December, 1933), 411—13. Although the masthead showed Shillaber and S. W. Wilder as coeditors, there is every evidence that Shillaber alone performed the editorial duties.

16. "To the Reader," *Carpet Bag,* I (March 29, 1851), 5.
17. "Something New," *Carpet Bag,* II(March 12, 1853), 4.
18. "Experiences During Many Years," *New England Magazine,* IX (October, 1893), 157.
19. *Ibid.,* p. 154.
20. *Ibid.,* p. 157.
21. Bungay, p. 376.
22. Boston *Post,* December 13, 1855.
23. "Mrs. Partington on the Union," Boston *Saturday Evening Gazette,* December 22, 1860.
24. Boston *Saturday Evening Gazette,* April 27, 1861.
25. *Ibid.,* October 11, 1862.
26. "Experiences During Many Years," *New England Magazine,* X (April, 1894), 250.
27. Bungay, p. 372.
28. Letter to B. P. Shillaber from unknown correspondent, March 7, 1871 (Brown University Library).
29. Robert J. Greef, "Public Lectures in New York, 1851—1878: A Cultural Index of the Times" (unpublished Ph.D. dissertation, University of Chicago, 1941), p. 203 n.
30. Letter from B. P. Shillaber to Mrs. Morris P. Ferris, April 3, 1889 (University of Virginia Library).
31. "Experiences During Many Years," *New England Magazine,* X (April, 1894), 254.
32. Letter from B. P. Shillaber to unknown correspondent, February 21, 1879 (Chicago Historical Society Library).
33. Letter from B. P. Shillaber to Mrs. Morris P. Ferris, April 3, 1889 (University of Virginia Library).
34. John T. Trowbridge, *My Own Story, with Recollections of Noted Persons* (Boston and New York, 1903), p. 180.

Chapter Two

1. For a full discussion of the vernacular tradition see Richard Bridgman, *The Colloquial Style in America* (New York, 1966).
2. "Experiences During Many Years," *New England Magazine,* IX (September, 1893), 94.
3. *Life and Sayings of Mrs. Partington, and Others of the Family*

(New York and Boston, 1854) pp. 2—46. Hereafter referred to as *Sayings*.
4. *Ibid.*, pp. vii—viii.
5. Boston *Saturday Evening Gazette*, May 5, 1860.
6. Letter to E. S. Marsh, July 30, 1884 (Yale University Library).
7. "Mrs. Partington and Graham," *Carpet Bag*, II (February 19, 1853), 4.
8. *New England Magazine*, IX (September 1893), 94—95.
9. "Appointing Inspectors," *Sayings*, pp. 78—79.
10. "Fancy Diseases," *Sayings*, p. 72.
11. "Mrs. Partington at Tea.," *Sayings*, p. 79.
12. Boston *Post*, April 5, 1848.
13. "An Inquiry Answered," *Sayings*, p. 159.
14. *Partingtonian Patchwork* (New York and Boston, 1873), p. 174. Hereafter referred to as *Patchwork*.
15. *Carpet Bag*, II (January 22, 1853), 2.
16. *Sayings*, p. 105.
17. "Antiquity in a Shower," *Sayings*, pp. 120—21.
18. Boston *Post*, June 24, 1847.
19. *Ibid.*, June 19, 1847.
20. *Ibid.*, June 14, 1854.
21. "A Little Truth Well Put," *Sayings*, pp. 68—69.
22. "Oracular Pearls," *Patchwork*, p. 168.
23. "Excellent Advice," *Sayings*, p. 339.
24. "Mrs. Partington at the Play," *Sayings*, p. 349.
25. "Mrs. Partington at the Ballet," *Mrs. Partington's Knitting Work and What Was Done by Her Plaguy Boy Ike; A Web of Many Textures, as Wrought by the Old Lady Herself* (Philadelphia, 1868), p. 48. Hereafter referred to as *Knitting Work*.
26. Boston *Post*, August 7, 1847.
27. "The Cat and the Kittens," *Sayings*, p. 109.
28. Boston *Saturday Evening Gazette*, March 20, 1858.
29. Boston *Post*, June 28, 1847.
30. "Eternal Indebtedness," *Sayings*, p. 246.
31. Boston *Post*, January 20, 1849.
32. "Torchlight Patriotism," *Saying*, pp. 165—66.
33. "By Chance," *Knitting Work*, pp. 40—41.
34. Boston *Post*, September 27, 1853.
35. *Ibid.*, April 5, 1854.
36. "On Elocution," *Sayings*, pp. 255—56.
37. "Operatic Rebuke," *Sayings*, p. 293.
38. Boston *Post*, October 29, 1847.
39. "A Striking Manifestation," *Sayings*, p. 83.
40. "Mrs. Partington and Piety," *Sayings*, p. 236.

41. Boston *Post*, June 8, 1855.
42. *Ibid.*, November 11, 1854.
43. *Ibid.*, September 26, 1848.
44. "A Home Truth," *Sayings*, p. 162.
45. "Mrs. Partington on the Union," Boston *Saturday Evening Gazette*, December 22, 1860.
46. *Mrs. Partington's New Grip Sack, Filled with Fresh Things* (New York, 1890), p. 209.
47. *The Drummer, or New York Clerks and Country Merchants* (Milwaukee, 1851).
48. Samuel P. Avery, *Mrs. Partington's Carpet Bag of Fun* (New York, 1854).

Chapter Three

1. "A Porcine Exposure," *Sayings*, p. 146.
2. "Old Roger and the Boarders," *Sayings*, p. 369.
3. *Ibid.*, p. 326.
4. Boston *Post*, November 24, 1847.
5. *Sayings*, p. 218.
6. Boston *Post*, January 29, 1848.
7. Boston *Saturday Evening Gazette*, April 2, 1859, p. 2.
8. *Ibid.*, June 23, 1860, p. 2.
9. *Ibid.*, October 9, 1858, p. 1.
10. *Ibid.*, December 11, 1858, p. 1.
11. *Ibid.*, February 12, 1859, p. 4.
12. "Individuality," *Knitting Work*, p. 56.
13. "Who Is Vile? ", *Knitting Work*, pp. 42–43.
14. "The Modern Syntax; Dr. Spooner in Search of the Delectable," *Patchwork*, p. 147.
15. "Industry," Boston *Saturday Evening Gazette*, March 5, 1859, p. 1.
16. "Blifkins the Mechanic," *Patchwork*, pp. 26–29.
17. "Blifkins' Summer Retreat," *Patchwork*, pp. 12–22.
18. "Blifkins the Householder," *Patchwork*, pp. 24–25.
19. "Blifkins and the Cat," *Patchwork*, pp. 29–34.
20. "Blifkins the Horticulturist," *Patchwork*, pp. 77–81.
21. "Blifkins Takes a Stand," *Patchwork*, pp. 93–94.
22. "Blifkins the Mourner," *Patchwork*, pp. 54–55.
23. "Blifkins Sees Kean," *Patchwork*, p. 61.
24. The name of the character also appears in various places in his writings as "Widesworth" and "Wide-Swath."

25. *Rhymes With Reason and Without* (Boston, 1853), p. 305.
Hereafter referred to as *Rhymes*.
26. "To Spring," *Rhymes*, p. 305
27. "Sunset," *Rhymes*, pp. 326–27.
28. "Church Music," *Rhymes*, p. 304.
29. "On a Picture of Lillie," *Rhymes*, p. 301.
30. "Lips," *Rhymes*, pp. 318–19.
31. "In Strange Company," *Rhymes*, p. 306.
32. "The Dance," *Rhymes*, pp. 320–21.
33. "Friendship," *Rhymes*, p. 309.
34. "Webster vs. Wideswarth," *Rhymes*, p. 335.
35. "Riding," *Rhymes*, p. 316.
36. "Philanthropy," *Rhymes*, p. 318.

Chapter Four

1. For information about Samuel G. Goodrich see Alice M. Jordon, *From Rollo to Tom Sawyer and Other Papers* (Boston, 1948), pp. 61–72.
2. For information about Jacob Abbott see Jordon, pp. 72–81.
3. *New England Magazine*, IX (October 1893), 153.
4. "Bringing Up Children," *Knitting Work*, p. 106.
5. Boston *Post*, December 22, 1854.
6. "Paul's Ghost," *Sayings*, pp. 51–53.
7. "Mrs. Partington Ruralizing," *Sayings*, pp. 174–75.
8. "A Prediction," *Sayings*, p. 201.
9. "The China Question," *Sayings*, pp. 49–50.
10. "Fourth of July," *Sayings*, pp. 352–53.
11. "Ike and the Elephant," *Sayings*, p. 201.
12. "Ike and Lion," *Knitting Work*, pp. 300–301.
13. "Ike in the Country," *Sayings*, pp. 257–58.
14. "How Ike Dropped the Cat," *Sayings*, pp. 91–93.
15. "Ike So Tender-Hearted," *Sayings*, p. 54.
16. This must surely be the book which Shillaber had in mind. It was published by F. Gleason, Boston, in 1847.
17. "Down with the Tyrant," *Sayings*, pp. 167–68.
18. "The Largest Liberty," *Sayings*, p. 65.
19. "Ike at Church," *Knitting Work*, p. 149.
20. "Wholesome Advice," *Sayings*, p. 86.
21. "Mrs. Partington on Vacation," *Sayings*, p. 164.
22. "The Guardian for Ike," *Knitting Work*, pp. 26–27.
23. *Ike Partington; or, The Adventures of a Human Boy and His Friends* (Boston, 1879), pp. 3–4. Hereafter referred to as *Ike Partington*.
24. *Ike Partington*, p. 225.

25. "Preface," *Cruises with Captain Bob on Sea and Land* (Boston, 1880), p. ix.

26. "Explanatory," *The Double-Runner Club; or, The Lively Boys of Riverton* (Boston, 1882), p. 5. Hereafter referred to as *Double-Runner Club.*

27. *Double-Runner Club*, pp. 84–87.

28. *Ibid.*, pp. 225–33.

29. *Ibid.*, pp. 193–205.

30. *Ibid.*, pp. 123–33.

31. *Ibid.*, pp. 285–88.

Chapter Five

1. "A Life's Fortunes," *Knitting Work*, p. 339.

2. "Missing," *Patchwork*, pp. 314–15.

3. "A New Year's Revery," *Patchwork*, pp. 330–45.

4. "Christmas Hearth and Hearts," Boston *Saturday Evening Gazette*, December 27, 1856.

5. *Rhymes*, pp. [v]–vi.

6. Boston *Post*, March 12, 1850.

7. "A Glance Out into the Cool," *Rhymes*, pp. 117–19.

8. "The Cottage by the Sea," *Rhymes* pp. 143–45.

9. "Ballad of the Piscataqua," *Rhymes*, pp. 21–23.

10. "The Witch of Lynn: or, a Good Many Years Ago," *Rhymes*, pp. 218–20.

11. "The Quilting," *Lines*, pp. 235–37.

12. "The Old Time Apple Bee," *Lines*, pp. 244–46.

13. "Music of the Flail," *Lines*, pp. 268–69.

14. "The Old Stage-Coach," *Lines*, pp. 285–86.

15. "Apples: An Analogy," *Rhymes*, p. 221.

16. "A Sweet Revenge," *Rhymes*, pp. 135–37.

17. "The Consumptive," *Rhymes*, pp. 47–48.

18. "On the Death of a Child," *Rhymes*, pp. 146–47.

19. "Parson Storer in a Fix; or, the Magic of a Kiss Misapplied," *Rhymes*, pp. 138–42.

20. "The Song of the Jilted One," *Rhymes*, pp. 49–51.

21. "Mrs. Partington at Tea," *Rhymes*, pp. 73–74.

22. "Mrs. Partington's Farewell When She Left the *Post*," *Rhymes*, pp. 77–79.

23. "Oracular Pearls Gathered from the Lips of Mrs. Partington," *Rhymes*, pp. 276–77.

24. "What Was It All About?" *Carpet Bag*, I (October 25, 1851), 4.

25. "New Hampshire," *Rhymes*, pp. 92–93.

26. "Home Again," *Lines*, pp. 26–34.
27. "Experiences During Many Years," *New England Magazine*, IX (December 1893), 531.
28. "Twenty Years Later," *Lines*, pp. 35–42.
29. "The Mound Builders," *Lines*, pp. 13–25.
30. "Twenty-One," *Lines*, pp. 43–51.
31. "A Hundred Years Ago," *Lines*, pp. 94–103.
32. "Experiences During Many Years," *New England Magazine*, X (April 1894), 254.
33. "Press and Press People," *Lines*, pp. 86–89.
34. "Welcome to Jenny Lind," *Rhymes*, pp. 130–31.
35. "Congratulatory," *Lines*, pp. 157–58.
36. "Daniel Webster Is No More," *Rhymes*, pp. 183–84.
37. "Miles O'Reilly," *Lines*, pp. 224–26.
38. "War Lyrics," *Lines*, pp. 133–48.

Chapter Six

1. "Experiences During Many Years," *New England Magazine*, X (March 1894), 33.
2. "The Bright Side of Life: A Lecture By Mrs. Partington," New York *Tribune*, December 14, 1859.
3. Miriam Rossiter Small, *Oliver Wendell Holmes* (New York, 1965), pp. 70–71.
4. Greef, p. 203.
5. Letter from Shillaber to H. H. Bigelow, September 14, n. y. (New York Public Library).
6. Evansville (Indiana) *Daily Journal*, December 5, 1857.
7. Cleveland *Leader*, November 23, 1857; Chicago *Press*, November 27, 1857; Cincinnati *Gazette*, December 2, 1857; Evansville *Daily Journal*, December 5, 1857; Clarksville (Tenn.) *Chronicle*, December 11, 1857; Boston *Saturday Evening Gazette*, December 5, 1857–January 16, 1858.
8. *New England Magazine*, X (April 1894), 249–50.
9. Clarksville (Tenn.) *Chronicle*, December 11, 1857.
10. Cincinnati *Enquirer*, December 2, 1857.
11. Letter from Shillaber to H. H. Bigelow, September 14, n. y. (New York Public Library).
12. Boston *Post*, December 13, 1855, January 26, and February 12, 1856.
13. Clarksville (Tenn.) *Chronicle*, December 11, 1857.
14. Melville D. Landon, *Kings of the Platform and Pulpit* (Chicago, 1896), pp. 425–30.
15. New York *Tribune*, December 14, 1859.

16. Evansville (Indiana) *Daily Journal,* December 5, 1857.
17. Cincinnati *Gazette,* December 2, 1857.

Chapter Seven

1. Quoted in the Boston *Post,* December 7, 1853.
2. Quoted in Boston *Saturday Evening Gazette,* August 20, 1859.
3. *Harper's Magazine,* IX (June 1854), 136.
4. Bungay, p. 373.
5. *Harper's Weekly,* XXXIV (December 6, 1890), 951.
6. "Benjamin Penhallow Shillaber," *New England Magazine,* IV (June 1891), 428–34.
7. *The Cambridge History of American Literature,* ed. William P. Trent *et al.,* II (New York, 1917), 155.
8. Jennette Tandy, *Crackerbox Philosophers in American Humor and Satire* (New York, 1925), p. 132.
9. Franklin J. Meine, "The Carpet Bag," *The Collector's Journal,* IV (October–December, 1933), 411–13.
10. *American Humor,* pp. 49–51, 57–58.
11. Walter Blair, *Horse Sense in American Humor from Benjamin Franklin to Ogden Nash* (Chicago, 1942), pp. 229–30.
12. *American Humor,* pp. 150–53.
13. "Experiences During Many Years," *New England Magazine,* IX (October 1893), 154.

Selected Bibliography

Very little of Shillaber's writing has been collected and undoubtedly some of it has not even been identified. A large body of his work, perhaps the bulk of it, is contained in three periodicals: The *Carpet Bag*, 1851–53; the Boston *Post*, 1847–50, 1853–56; and the Boston *Saturday Evening Gazette*, 1856–67.

The only bibliographies of the books and articles by and about Shillaber are those found in Walter Blair's *Native American Humor 1800–1900* and in Cyril Clemens's *Shillaber*. These two bibliographies are far from complete.

Manuscripts of sketches by Shillaber are rare, but letters are fairly plentiful. The listing in Joseph Jones, ed., *American Literary Manuscripts* (Austin, 1960), is very helpful.

PRIMARY SOURCES

Mrs. Partington's New Grip Sack, Filled with Fresh Things. New York: J. S. Ogilvie, 1890.

Partingtonian Patchwork. Boston: Lee and Shepard; New York: Lee, Shepard and Dillingham, 1872.

Rhymes, with Reason and Without. Boston: Abel Tompkins and B. B. Mussey and Company, 1853.

The Sayings and Doings of the Celebrated Mrs. Partington, ("Relic" of Corporal P. P.) and Others of the Family. London: James Blackwood, 1854. An abridged British edition of *The Life and Sayings of Mrs. Partington and Others of the Family*.

"Lively Boys! Lively Boys!" Ike Partington; or, The Adventures of a Human Boy and His Friends. Boston: Lee and Shepard; New York: Charles T. Dillingham, 1879.

A Midnight Race. Boston: Ticknor and Co., 1888.

Mrs. Partington's Grab Bag. The Contents of Which Are Very, Very

Funny. New York: F. M. Lupton, 1893. Reissue of *Mrs. Partington's New Grip Sack.*

Mrs. Partington's Knitting Work; and What Was Done by Her Plaguy Boy Ike. A Web of Many Textures, as Wrought by the Old Lady Herself. Philadelphia: John E. Potter and Company, 1868. A reissue of the 1859 *Knitting-Work.*

Mrs. Partington's Ridicule. A Collection of Wit and Humor, Which the Old Lady Offers to Her Friends. Ten Cent Novelettes No. 86. Boston: Thomes and Talbot 1863.

Cruises With Captain Bob on Sea and Land. Boston: Lee and Shepard; New York: Charles T. Dillingham, 1880.

The Double-Runner Club; or, the Lively Boys of Riverton. Boston: Lee and Shepard; New York: Charles T. Dillingham, 1882.

"Experiences During Many Years," *New England Magazine,* VIII (1893), 511–25, 618–27, 719–24; IX (1893), 88–95, 153–60, 529–33, 625–31; X (1894), 29–36, 247–56, 286–94.

Knitting-Work: A Web of Many Textures, Wrought by Ruth Partington. Boston: Brown, Taggard and Chase; New York: Sheldon and Co., 1859. Reissued as *Mrs. Partington's Knitting Work* in 1868.

Life and Sayings of Mrs. Partington and Others of the Family. New York: J. C. Derby; Boston: Phillips, Samson, and Company; Cincinnati: H. W. Derby, 1854.

Lines in Pleasant Places: Rhythmics of Many Moods and Quantities. Wise and Otherwise. Chelsea, Mass.: The Author, 1874. Reissued in 1882 as *Wide-Swath.*

Wide-Swath. Embracing Lines in Pleasant Places and Other Rhymes Wise and Otherwise. Cambridge: Moses King, 1882. A reissue of *Lines in Pleasant Places,* 1874.

SECONDARY SOURCES

ANON. "Benjamin P. Shillaber," *Harper's Weekly,* XXXIV (December 6, 1890), 951. Brief assessment of Shillaber's accomplishment as a humorist written soon after his death.

————. "The Original Mrs. Partington," *Every Saturday,* X (April 29, 1871), 394. Account of Sydney Smith's famous speech containing an anecdote about a Mrs. Partington in Sidmouth, Devonshire.

————. Review of *The Life and Sayings of Mrs. Partington, Harper's Magazine,* IX (June, 1854), 136. Lively review stresses the merits of the characterization and style of the Partington sketches.

————. Review of *The Life and Sayings of Mrs. Partington, Peterson's Magazine,* XXV (June, 1854), 409.

ALLAN, ELIZABETH AKERS. "Benjamin Penhallow Shillaber,"

New England Magazine, IV (June, 1891), 428–34. Panegyric written soon after Shillaber's death; contains a good biographical summary.

AUSTIN, JAMES C. *Artemus Ward.* New York: Twayne Publishers Inc., 1964. Discussion of Shillaber and the *Carpet Bag.*

BLAIR, WALTER. *Horse Sense in American Humor from Benjamin Franklin to Ogden Nash.* Chicago: University of Chicago Press, 1942. Examines Shillaber's humor in the context of the common-sense tradition in American humor.

————. *Mark Twain and Huck Finn.* Berkeley and Los Angeles: University of California Press, 1960. Examination of Shillaber's influence on Clemens.

————. *Native American Humor.* New York: American Book Company, 1937. Excellent scholarly assessment of Shillaber's achievement as a humorist.

BUNGAY, GEORGE W. *Off-Hand Takings; or Crayon Sketches of the Noticeable Men of Our Age.* New York: DeWitt and Davenport, 1854. Good study by a contemporary of Shillaber as a personality.

CLEMENS, CYRIL. "Benjamin Shillaber and His 'Carpet Bag,' " *New England Quarterly,* XIV (September, 1941), 519–37. Useful factual account of the *Carpet Bag* venture.

————. *Shillaber.* Webster Groves, Missouri: International Mark Twain Society, 1946. Useful but not very scholarly biography of Shillaber.

COLEMAN, RUFUS A. "Trowbridge and Shillaber," the *New England Quarterly,* XX (June, 1947), 232–46. Examination of the relationship between Shillaber and Trowbridge; comparison of their work.

DERBY, JAMES C. *Fifty Years Among Authors, Books, and Publishers.* New York: G. W. Carleton and Company, 1886. Includes a letter from Shillaber concerning the publication of *The Life and Sayings of Mrs. Partington* in 1854.

LANDON, MELVILLE D. *Kings of the Platform and Pulpit.* Chicago: F. C. Smedley and Company, 1891. Biographical details on Shillaber; text of a lecture purported to be by him.

MEINE, FRANKLIN J. "American Comic Periodicals. No. 1—The Carpet Bag," *The Collector's Journal,* IV (October, November, December, 1933), 411–13. Detailed account of the *Carpet Bag.*

————. "Benjamin Penhallow Shillaber," *Dictionary of American Biography.* Competent summary of his life and career as a humorist.

MOTT, FRANK LUTHER. *American Journalism.* New York: Macmillan, 1941. Information on the Boston *Post.*

————. *A History of American Magazines.* Cambridge: Harvard University Press, 1938. Material on the *Carpet Bag.*

ROURKE, CONSTANCE. *American Humor: A Study of the National Character.* Anchor Book. New York: Doubleday and Company, Inc., n.d. Contains an excellent discussion of New England humor.

TANDY, JENNETTE. *Crackerbox Philosophers in American Humor and Satire.* New York: Columbia University Press, 1925. One of the earliest and best studies of the tradition of native American humor.

TROWBRIDGE, JOHN TOWNSEND. *My Own Story with Recollections of Noted Persons.* Boston and New York: Houghton Mifflin and Company, 1903. Reminiscences of Shillaber by a fellow writer who knew him well.

Index